TO: Opal

Best Wish

Mike Vie

Varsity Sports at Indiana University

Varsity Sports at Indiana University

A *Pictorial History*

by Cecil K. Byrd and Ward W. Moore

Indiana University Press

Bloomington & Indianapolis

This book is a publication of
Indiana University Press
601 North Morton Street
Bloomington, IN 47404–3797 USA

http://www.indiana.edu/~iupress

Telephone orders   800–842–6796
Fax orders   812–855–7931
Orders by e-mail   iuporder@indiana.edu

The paper used in this publication meets the minimum
requirements of American National Standard for Information
Sciences—Permanence of Paper for Printed Library Materials,
ANSI Z39.48–1984.

MANUFACTURED IN THE UNITED STATES OF AMERICA

Library of Congress Cataloging-in-Publication Data

Byrd, Cecil K.
     Varsity sports at Indiana University : a pictorial history /
Cecil K. Byrd and Ward W. Moore.
          p.   cm.
     Includes index.
     ISBN 0-253-33578-7 (cl : alk. paper)
     1. Indiana University—Sports—History. 2. Indiana
University, Bloomington—Sports—History. 3. Indiana
University—Sports—History Pictorial works. 4. Indiana
University, Bloomington—Sports—History Pictorial
works.   I. Moore, Ward W.   II. Title.
GV691.I63B97   1999
796.04'3'09772255—dc21   99-12930

1 2 3 4 5 04 03 02 01 00 99

To Esther and Fran

Contents

Preface

At the time this work was initially contemplated, the authors were not aware of any single publication that depicted each and every one of the intercollegiate athletic programs at Indiana University. This pictorial history of varsity sports at IU is intended to fill that void.

We planned a project which we hoped would be similar to and as comprehensive as an earlier book authored by Dorothy C. Collins and Cecil K. Byrd, *Indiana University: A Pictorial History,* which had been published by Indiana University Press in 1992. After receiving a favorable response to this new project from John Gallman, Director of the Press, in the fall of 1996, we consulted Clarence Doninger, Director of Intercollegiate Athletics at IU, and personnel at the University Archives. All agreed to cooperate with us. Our work was delayed when Dr. Byrd's health deteriorated in February of 1997. Two months after his untimely death on April 16, 1997, with the concurrence of the others involved in the project, as well as Dr. Byrd's family, I resumed the work alone.

Our early efforts had focused on how to proceed. The work had been divided, and searches for information were under way. Early drafts of the manuscript, as well as proposals and agreements for the use of proposed photographs, were in progress, but had not been completed. We had not yet begun our search for the photographs themselves prior to Dr. Byrd's death. I made the final selection of photographs, and wrote the accompanying captions, with the able assistance of Bradley Cook and John Gallman.

The sources for the information in this book include the University Archives, the files of the Indiana University Sports Information Office (including media guides, managers' notebooks, game programs and statistics, and photographs), the *Arbutus,* microfilms in the University Library of the *Student,* the *Indiana Student,* and the *Indiana Daily Student,* the files of the Indiana University Alumni Association, the University Photographic Services, and the latest records published by the Big Ten Conference. At times we were hampered in our efforts to track down appropriate photographs pertaining to the 130-year period covered by the project. Pictures of some of IU's outstanding teams and athletes could not be obtained, and some individuals in group photographs could not be properly identified.

We are indebted to many individuals and offices of the University and in the community of Bloomington. Bradley Cook of the University Archives has been indispensable to the project. His ideas, searches, data collection, and general expertise have been invaluable. Philip Bantin and Tom Malefatto of the University Archives have been extremely helpful. Thanks also to the Department of Intercollegiate Athletics, including Clarence Doninger, Isabella Hutchison, David Martin, Chuck Crabb, Kit Klingelhoffer, Beth Feichert, Shelli Stewart, Greg Elkin, and Debbie O'Leary. Several student interns who serve on Mr. Klingelhoffer's media relations staff were of great help. They are Ryan Frantz, Greg Greenwell, Ryan Margulis, Sarah Melton, Becky Parke, Jason Parry, Josh Rawitch, and David Shepley. Becky Batman, Lauren Bryant, Claude Rich, Eugene Fletchall, Tom Bolyard, and John Laskowski of the Alumni Office made significant contributions.

We would also like to acknowledge the help of John Pfeifer, a collector of IU sports memorabilia, and to thank Mrs. Vern Huffman for permitting us to use the photograph of her late husband's Most Valuable Player award. Great help came from Teresa Webb, Sharon Leigh, Shelly Nelson, Christy Neilsen, and Steve Wier at the Indiana University Photographic Services. Most of the recent photographs used in the book were taken by IU Photographic Service photographers Guy Zimmer, Nick Judy, Mark Simons, Beverly Simpson, Paul Riley, and Kevin Kleine. Dean Tony Mobley and Dr. Kay Burrus in the School of HPER, as well as Aline Robinson and Chuck Peters, were also great sources of information. We would also like to thank Diane Richardson and Margaret Zuckschwerdt of the Medical Sciences Program of the IU School of Medicine, Robert M. Stump, Jr., and his staff in the Office of Admissions of the School of Medicine, and Jeanne Hayes of the Office of the Dean of the School of Medicine for their help.

In the last eighty-five years, Indiana University varsity teams have won nearly 125 Big Ten championships, two dozen NCAA titles, and many hundreds of games and meets; individual athletes have won numerous Olympic medals, dozens of NCAA titles, and hundreds of Big Ten championships. We regret that we did not have room to include images of all of IU's outstanding performers over the years. We apologize for our omissions.

The book covers the period from 1867 though calendar year 1997, and is arranged according to the date that each sport gained varsity and intercollegiate status.

—Ward W. Moore

The first gymnasium on campus was completed on January 20, 1892. The 40' x 50' structure cost $1,000. It was located north of Owen Hall and south of the present Union Building. In 1895, bathroom facilities that could accommodate eight people at a time were added to the building. When the New Gymnasium (Old Assembly Hall) was completed in 1897, the first gymnasium became the carpenter shop. It was razed in 1932.

Introduction

Intercollegiate athletics at Indiana University began soon after the end of the Civil War, as students formed clubs in connection with several athletic activities. In those days, students participated in sporting events for the fun of it—unlike many of today's athletes, who view college sports as a steppingstone to the high-paying world of professional sports. The academic community, at first reluctant, gradually became more receptive to the idea and began to take a more active part. University alumni also became increasingly involved, eventually pushing hard for their favored athletic program. They donated money, and they also demanded success, which was attained in some sports, but not in others. Success meant an increase in the costs to be borne by the university in support of sports programs, and the recruitment of players quickly became competitive.

Athletics have played a large part in the life of IU over the years, fostering pride at the institution itself and among the citizens of the state. Sports programs have created a cohesiveness among students, faculty, and alumni.

The progress of individual athletes and team sports on the Bloomington campus has been variable. The Hoosier basketball, soccer, swimming and diving, women's golf and tennis, and track and field and cross country teams have had their share of success, while alumni and fans have endured the relative lack of success of the football, baseball, gymnastics, volleyball, men's golf, field hockey, and wrestling squads.

Indiana University at Bloomington supports twenty intercollegiate varsity sports programs, in which approximately 500 student athletes participate. Coaching and support staffs numbering more than 100 people prepare and guide these athletes—a coach/athlete ratio higher than the mentor/student ratio in the university's academic programs. There are ten varsity sports for men—baseball, football, track and field, tennis, cross country, basketball, wrestling, swimming and diving, golf, and soccer—involving about 330 male student athletes a year. Ten varsity programs are also currently available for women. As many as 170 female athletes participate annually in basketball, track and field, swimming and diving, cross country, golf, tennis, softball, volleyball, soccer, and water polo. (Women's water polo debuted as a varsity sport during the second semester of the 1997/98 school year.) At one time, IU also sponsored varsity teams in men's gymnastics (1914–1982) and rifle (1952–1957) and women's field hockey (1962–1982; to be reintroduced in 2000) and gymnastics (1968–1985). Most, if not all, of these varsity sports were preceded by active, sometimes very successful, student clubs, most of which were not supported, either directly or indirectly, by the university. Club activities that have not been advanced to varsity sports include archery, badminton, bowling, boxing, fencing, ice hockey, lacrosse, and rugby.

Indiana's sports teams are known by a number of nicknames: the Hoosiers, the Fighting Hoosiers, the Cream and Crimson, the Hurrying Hoosiers, the Scramblin' Hoosiers, and the Big Red. "Hoosier," a word of unknown origin, has been used since the early 1800s to designate a person from Indiana. "Cream and Crimson" traces back to the IU class of 1888, who produced an enlarged number of the *Student,* a monthly campus news publication, in a cream and crimson binding. These have been the official colors of Indiana University ever since. "Hurrying Hoosiers" was introduced by the *Indiana Daily Student,* and "Scramblin' Hoosiers" by the *Arbutus.* "Big Red" derives from the crimson in "Cream and Crimson."

Shortly after the end of the Civil War, Indiana University, under President Cyrus Nutt, began its gradual transition from a very small literary and oratorical student body to one that took more of an interest in physical fitness and athletic activities. In 1867, the institution experienced several changes: the first edition of the *Student,* a monthly newspaper, went to press on George Washington's birthday; for the first time, women were admitted to studies on an equal basis with men; the Indiana General Assembly made its first annual appropriation of funds, $8,000, for the operation of the university; and the University Baseball Club was formed by a group of students. The students submitted a request to the faculty on April 20, 1867, for permission to use the flat ground at the southeast corner of the campus for a baseball diamond. (In 1867, campus was located between Walnut and College Avenues and First and Second Streets south of the Courthouse Square.) Home plate was placed near the corner of Walnut and First Street. The student body at that time numbered slightly more than a hundred, and the total number of professors was eight.

Over the next decade, as baseball became more popular, the number of baseball clubs increased; but it was not until 1883 that the first truly intercollegiate athletic contest was staged at Indiana University: an extramural baseball game against Asbury College (later DePauw University) of Greencastle. The contest, played at the University Athletic Field on the Seminary Square campus, was won by Asbury, 23 to 6. That same year, a fire destroyed Science

Hall on the Seminary Square campus, and the university purchased Dunn's Woods, a tract of land located a few blocks east of the county courthouse. The following year, Owen Hall and Wylie Hall were erected in the northeast portion of what would later be called the Old Crescent.

Two years later, in 1886, during the second year of the presidency of David Starr Jordan, football made its first appearance on the IU campus. The April 1887 edition of the *Indiana Student* lamented, "Why the Board of Trustees has never given us a gymnasium is a question that has been much discussed among the students. The need of one is keenly felt, and there has been some talk of organizing an association for the purpose of equipping a hall down town where students may get needful exercise during inclement weather. Baseball and football are engaged spasmodically during certain seasons of the year, but as soon as the game is over there is no more practice until the eve of another game. Hence our boys are sometimes defeated when with the proper training might come off victorious." The Jordan administration began a fund drive for the construction of a gymnasium, and the program that would lead to the building of Gymnasium Hall was approved by the Board of Trustees on August 1, 1889.

Indiana University established the Department of Physical Training for Women in 1890, providing gymnasium space in the basement of Wylie Hall. The gymnasium space was moved to Mitchell Hall in 1896. In 1891, the Department of Physical Training for Men was formed, with gymnasium space made available in the basement of Owen Hall. That same year, according to Woodburn, the Athletic Association was organized at IU, with William E. Jenkins as president, John C. Capron as vice-president, Carl E. Wood as secretary, and James E. Hagerty as treasurer.

Following the construction of the Student Building in 1906, the Department of Physical Training for Women was moved there. The building included a large (80' x 50'), well-equipped gymnasium with a balcony on three sides, locker and dressing rooms, and a galvanized swimming pool (40' x 18', with a depth of 3'8").

The Formation of Athletic Organizations

In April 1888, six of the colleges and universities in Indiana formed the State Athletic Association, for the primary purpose of organizing and monitoring athletic programs within their institutions. Those six schools were Indiana University, Butler University, DePauw University, Hanover College, Purdue University, and Wabash College.

For many years there were few, if any, rules or regulations concerning athletic competition between teams at American colleges and universities. In the 1890s, universities tended to be concerned with only three sports: baseball, football, and track and field. Most coaches were employed seasonally—some for only the weekend. The term "tramp athlete" was in common usage; "ringers" were used; and there might be a "playing coach." There were no rules about the number of years a "student" could

First used in 1898, **Jordan Field** served as the venue for football and track meets until 1925; baseball was played there until 1951, when the games were moved to the diamond that became Sembower Field. Jordan Field also functioned as a parade ground for the ROTC, as shown in this photo.

participate in collegiate sports; Walter Camp, the "Dean of American Football," played football at Yale University for six years. In many instances athletes were not even enrolled at the college they represented on the athletic field. Games were frequently halted when a team decided to quit the field of play. Many games were badly managed and officiated, and indifference and opposition—sometimes even hostility—to sports on the part of the faculty frequently meant that the management of athletic contests was left to interested students.

In response to this growing problem, the president of Purdue University, James H. Smart, invited the presidents of six other midwestern institutions to a meeting in Chicago on January 11, 1895, to discuss the state of their athletic programs and contests and to propose some means of bringing some order to them. The universities represented were the University of Chicago, the University of Illinois, Lake Forest University, the University of Minnesota, Northwestern University, Purdue University, and the University of Wisconsin. Conway McMillin of Minnesota chaired the group. At this initial meeting, rules and guidelines were drawn up that placed restrictions on the eligibility of students involved in athletic contests: only full-time students who were not delinquent in their studies could

compete in intercollegiate athletic events; athletes were prohibited from receiving gifts or remuneration; and the use of an assumed name was forbidden. On February 8, 1896, the seven "faculty representatives" met in Chicago, calling themselves the Intercollegiate Conference of Faculty Representatives. The "Big Seven" proceeded to draw up standards and to put the machinery in place for the control of intercollegiate athletics in their schools.

As the May 17, 1896, issue of *Harper's Weekly* noted, "The most notable clearing in the atmosphere is to be seen in the West. Football—indeed all Middle Western college sports—was very near total extinction last year because of a rampant professional spirit that had ranged throughout nearly all universities, leaving corruption in its wake. . . . The meeting last winter in Chicago marked the beginning of a new and clarified era in Western college sport." In 1900, this system would be strongly recommended to the leaders of eastern collegiate sports. At the Big Seven conference meeting on November 25, 1898, twelve more rules were added by the Athletic Committee, or Board of Control, which governed the activities of the members. Many more changes have been made since then, in connection with the dimensions of the playing areas, the rules of games, the eligibility of participants, permissible expenses, radio and television broadcasts, and participation of the member schools in bowl games.

In 1896, the University of Michigan replaced Lake Forest University in the conference. On December 1, 1899, Indiana University and the University of Iowa were admitted, and the former "Big Seven" became the "Big Nine." At the time there were 1,017 students enrolled on the Bloomington campus of IU. On January 14, 1908, Michigan withdrew from the conference, objecting to the "retroactive application [of the rules] to include those student-athletes already registered allowing only 3 years of play," a decision that affected the play of Michigan All-American lineman Al Benbrook. Ohio State University was admitted to the group in 1912. Michigan was readmitted in 1917, and the conference became the "Big Ten." The University of Chicago withdrew from the conference in 1946, to be replaced by Michigan State University three years later. Pennsylvania State University was admitted in 1990, but the eleven universities and the conference continue to be known as the "Big Ten."

During the latter part of the nineteenth century and the early twentieth century, many colleges and universities discontinued football. Numerous injuries and deaths had resulted from its rough and rugged play, which was typified by gang tackling and mass formations such as the flying wedge. Little if any protective gear was worn by the players. It was the opinion of many that either the game had to be reformed, or football should be eliminated from the college scene. In December of 1905, with the strong backing of several of the Big Nine schools and President Theodore Roosevelt, representatives from sixty-two schools met in New York City to discuss the issue. That meeting led to the founding on March 31, 1906, of the Intercollegiate Athletic Association of the United States (IAAUS), renamed the National Collegiate Athletic Association (NCAA) in 1910.

The NCAA, the regulatory and enforcement agency for college sports, strives to maintain the quality and amateur status of collegiate athletics through rigid enforcement of its rules. It has more than 800 members today, and is organized into five divisions: I, I-A, I-AA, II, and III. Three primary criteria determine membership in each of the divisions: (1) financial aid awards and requirements; (2) eligibility requirements of the athletes; and (3) the number of sports sponsored by the institutions, including the minimum number of sports supported, the minimum number of contests per sport per season, the number of participants in each sport, scheduling requirements of the individual sports, and student attendance at each athletic event. Indiana University is a member of Division I, the division with the largest number of members. The Big Ten Conference abides by the NCAA's rules and regulations, but it is allowed to legislate higher admission requirements and academic standards for its athletes than does the NCAA. Similarly, Indiana University can, and does, stipulate higher admission requirements and academic standards than do the Big Ten Conference and the NCAA. The Big Ten can also legislate on any sport not in conflict with the rules and regulations of the NCAA. It controls the scheduling of all games within the conference and negotiates bowl agreements.

Indiana athletes first entered Big Ten competition in 1900. That year the football team had a record of 1 win, 2 losses, and 1 tie, finishing seventh in a field of nine. In 1913/14, Coach Elmer Jones's wrestlers were the first team from IU to win a Big Ten championship. As of December 1997, IU's men's teams have vied for many titles in Big Ten competition, winning a total of 118 championships (18 of which were shared).

Indiana University strives for gender equity in all of its sports programs. Members of the women's basketball and field hockey teams were the first IU women to participate in intercollegiate sports, competing in a limited number of games within the state during the early 1960s. Later, in 1966, a women's volleyball team was organized, and it played a few games during the year. In 1967 the women's golf, tennis, and gymnastics teams became active (the gymnastics program was eliminated in 1985). Swimming and diving and softball programs were added in 1968. Indiana University became a member of the Association for Intercollegiate Athletics for Women (AIAW) in 1971, at which time the university spon-

Matthew Winters, a native of Poseyville, Indiana, was a tackle on the football team and a catcher on the baseball team. Edgar Davis and Sherman Minton were fellow members of the 1913 and 1914 squads. Winters earned the AB in 1915 and the AM in anatomy in 1917 at IU. He served as a captain in the infantry in World War I. After being discharged from the army, he earned the MD degree from the Rush Medical School in Chicago in 1921.

Winters joined the faculty of the IU School of Medicine in 1922 as an assistant in pediatrics, and in 1931 became the chairman of the Department of Pediatrics. He served as president of the IU Alumni Association from 1937 to 1939. After his retirement from the Medical School faculty in 1955, Winters was director of the Student Health Center on the Bloomington campus and a lecturer in the Department of Physiology. He died in 1958.

Golfer **Karen Marencik**, from Valparaiso, Indiana, was a medalist in the NIWGA tourney and a runner-up in the 1979 Women's Indiana State Amateur Tournament. She was co-medalist at the 1981 Indiana Invitational, shooting a 70 in the final round. During her last season, she averaged 79.8 strokes. In 1982, Marencik won the first women's Big Ten Medal of Honor.

sored eight women's sports. All competition was scheduled on Saturday, and the programs were operated on a meager budget. In most cases, the athletes had to furnish their own uniforms and equipment. Fund drives and donations plus extensive volunteer work were necessary to make the individual women's sports programs a success. Prior to 1971, teams were driven to away competition by parents, friends, and personnel in the Department of Physical Education in their own automobiles. Friends or parents of IU women athletes opened their homes to visiting players, coaches, and drivers. In the early years, none of the female student athletes received a grant-in-aid.

An amendment to the Higher Education Act of 1965, passed by the U.S. Congress in 1972, revolutionized women's athletic programs throughout the United States. Title IX, Section 901 (a) made a great stride forward in sports gender equity:

> No person in the United States shall, on the basis of sex, be excluded from participation in, be denied the benefits of, or be subjected to discrimination under any education program or activity receiving Federal financial assistance.

Indiana University responded to Title IX in 1974 by shifting the administration and financing of its women's sports programs from the Department of Physical Education for Women to the Department of Intercollegiate Athletics. The latter thus assumed responsibility for financing and administering the university's sports programs for women. In 1974, Leanne Grotke became Indiana's first full-time associate director for women's athletics. With this appointment, the university committed itself to supporting the appropriate development of its women's sports programs. Ms. Grotke was succeeded by interim director Ann Lawver in 1979. Isabella Hutchison became the director in 1980, and the current director, Mary Ann Rohleder, assumed her duties in 1995. In the fall of 1996, IU began offering grants-in-aid and athletic scholarships to women competing in eight sports. Twenty "full-ride" grants (tuition fees and room and board) became available for Indiana female student athletes. In August 1981, the Big Ten universities voted to affiliate the women's athletic programs within the conference. The University of Minnesota did not choose to affiliate at that time, but did so three months later.

One final step must be taken before gender equity is accomplished. The Big Ten has pledged to reach "a level of athletic participation that is 60% men and 40% women." The Big Ten universities will submit to the conference office strategies on how to achieve this commitment.

Awards for Athletes
According to the *IU Alumni Quarterly,* the first varsity "I" letter was awarded to Dick Miller of Indianapolis. To qualify for the Varsity "I" Award, a player must be a member in good standing of the team, practice

Mary Deputy earned the Maxwell Award in 1919 and was an outstanding performer as a member of the field hockey team and the swimming club. She earned both an AB and an MA in English in 1919.

Zora G. Clevenger is shown here with three of the first five winners of the Clevenger Award . From left to right: **Lloyd G. Balfour, Ralph N. Tirey**, Clevenger, and **Everett S. Dean**. George L. Fisher and Sherman Minton were unable to attend the ceremony.

Balfour was a native of Wauseon, Ohio, and graduated from Male High School in Louisville, Kentucky. He was awarded "I" letters in baseball in 1906 and 1907 and in football in 1906. In 1913 he founded the L. G. Balfour Company in Attleboro, Massachusetts, which became one of the leading jewelry companies in the nation, specializing in the making of fraternity and class rings. In 1929, he sponsored the Balfour Award, given to outstanding student athletes at Indiana. Balfour served as an officer in the IU Alumni Association. He was a Kentucky Colonel, a Tennessee Squire, an Admiral in the Texas Navy, an Admiral in the Nebraska Navy, and an Honorary Submariner, and was admitted to the Order of the Guppy Snorkelers by the U.S. Navy.

Tirey was a member of the baseball squad in 1918. He earned his BS in education, then, after serving as superintendent of schools in Lawrence County, earned his MS in 1928. He served as superintendent of the Bloomington School System and was elected president of the Indiana State Teachers Association in 1928. For several years he was a member of the IU Summer Session faculty. On January 15, 1934, he became the 64th Indiana University graduate to become a college president when he accepted the position at the Indiana State Teachers College in Terre Haute.

Dean was a native of Washington County, Indiana, and was an outstanding student, athlete, and coach at Indiana University. He was a three-year letterman in both basketball and baseball and coached teams in both of these sports at IU from 1925 to 1938.

regularly, complete the season as an eligible team member, and meet the minimum standards set by each sport. Awards may include a sweater, a jacket, or a coat with an "I," an "I" blanket, or a senior plaque. Varsity Awardees must be nominated by the head coach, and the nomination must be approved by the director of athletics and the University Athletics Committee.

Sigma Delta Psi, an athletic honorary society, was established in 1912 as a counterpart to the academic societies such as Phi Beta Kappa and Sigma Xi.

One year later, the "I" Men's Association was formed at a meeting prior to the Indiana–Illinois football game. Every athlete who had earned a varsity "I" was made a member of the association. "The purposes of the organization were to bind more closely together the men who had battled for the Cream and Crimson and to render service to the athletic programs at Indiana University in many and various ways." The organization's first officers were president, Carl E. Endicott (baseball, 1893–96); vice-president, Charles J. Sembower (baseball, 1891–94); and secretary, George M. Cook (football, 1895). Today the "I" Men's Association has more than 3,500 living members. Pat Connor of Indianapolis currently serves as its president.

The "I" Women's Association was formed in August of 1989, with 190 charter members, including nine coaches. Ginger Gilles, a native of Kokomo and a member of the 1979 softball and volleyball teams, has served as president of the organization since its founding. In June 1997, more than 200 women athletes who had participated in varsity sports from 1960 to 1977 were invited to a ceremony, at which each would be awarded, retroactively, a varsity "I" letter. Of those who received invitations, 90 attended the ceremony to receive their letters; an additional 65 women athletes have since received theirs.

The Big Ten Conference, emphasizing its support of educational activities for athletes, voted at its meeting of December 5, 1914, to set aside $2,000 for a Conference Medal of Honor, to be awarded to a senior who has "attained greatest proficiency in athletic and scholastic work." In 1915, Matthew Winters was IU's first recipient of this medal. In 1982, the Big Ten established a similar Medal of Honor for women. Karen Marencik was IU's first woman recipient.

The Gimbel Prize was instituted by Mr. Jake Gimbel of Vincennes in 1915. It awarded a gold medal and the annual interest on $500 for the "building of mental attitude in athletes . . . and was awarded for merit in habits, college spirit, application, and sincerity." The first winner was Claude M. Ewing.

In 1919, the first Maxwell Medal was awarded by the Women's Athletic Association. It honored "high scholarship, participation in University athletics, manners, neatness, speech, principles, sincerity, and sufficient attainment in physical training to have won an I. U. sweater." Mary Deputy was the first recipient. The medal was given in honor of Dr. James D. Maxwell, a distinguished president and member of the IU Board of Trustees for many years.

The Balfour Award, named for Lloyd G. Balfour, honors athletes for "conduct and play bringing honor and distinction to the University." It was first presented in 1929. The first recipients were Paul E. Harrell (baseball), Branch McCracken (basketball), Charles E. Bennett (football), Harold Fields (track), and Auree B. Scott (wrestling).

The Zora G. Clevenger Service Award, named for IU's first All-American and the athletic director of the univer-

George L. Fisher was an outstanding player on the 1923, 1924, and 1925 Indiana football teams. He also lettered in wrestling and track. After earning his BS in 1926, he played professional ball for a short time before returning to IU to earn a master's degree in 1931. He served as football coach (for 26 years), track coach (for 23 years), and baseball coach at Warsaw High School in Indiana. He also represented Kosciusko County in the Indiana State Legislature.

sity from 1923 to 1946, was first presented in 1963. The highest honor that the "I" Men's Association can bestow on one of its members, it is given to "living 'I' Men who, as alumni, have made outstanding contributions to Indiana University through service to its athletic program." The first Clevenger Award winners were Lloyd G. Balfour (LLB '07, LLD (hon) '66), Everett S. Dean (AB '21, MS '38), George L. Fisher (BS '26, MS '31), Sherman Minton (LLB '15, LLD (hon) '50), and Ralph N. Tirey (AB '18, AM '28, and LLD (hon) '45). Three awards have been given each year since 1963.

In 1982, the Big Ten athletic directors established the Big Ten–Jesse Owens Award, which honors the Big Ten Athlete of the Year. The first winner was Jim Spivey, an IU track and cross country star. Three other IU athletes have received this award: Sunder Nix (1984, track and field), Steve Alford (1987, basketball), and Anthony Thompson (1990, football). One year later, the Big Ten–Suzy Favor Athlete of the Year Award was established for the women athletes of the conference. The first recipient was Judi Brown, a member of the Michigan State track and field team.

That same year, the Altrusa Award of the Bloomington Chapter was presented to Amy McGrath, who distinguished herself in diving and scholarship. The first Aline Robinson Mental Attitude Award was presented to a

Sherman Minton, a native of Georgetown, Indiana, attended high school in New Albany before entering IU in 1911. He was a great hitter and outfielder on the baseball team and a halfback and rugged blocker in football, earning letters in both 1913 and 1914. Two other members of the baseball squad were Paul V. McNutt and Matthew Winters. "Shay," as Minton was called, worked his way through the university by waiting tables and playing semi-pro baseball. He was also an outstanding orator who earned an AB and a law degree at IU and an AM in law at Yale.

Minton served in France as an infantry captain during World War I. He returned to New Albany to practice law, becoming a successful attorney. He was appointed counsel to the Indiana Public Service Commission in 1932. Minton was active in the politics of the Democratic Party in Indiana. He is one of the few individuals who have served the nation in each of its three branches of government: he was elected to the United States Senate in 1934; he served as a special assistant to President Franklin D. Roosevelt in 1940/41; and he served as a judge on the U.S. Circuit Court of Appeals in Chicago (1941–49), and was appointed Justice of the United States Supreme Court by President Harry S Truman in 1949. Minton retired from his seat on the Supreme Court bench in 1956 because of ill health. He died at his home in New Albany in 1965, at the age of 74.

representative from each of the eight women's varsity sports in 1990. The Anita Aldrich Leadership Award was first presented in 1991 to Joy Jordan, an IU volleyball player. The Branch McCracken, Alvin "Bo" McMillin, and Arthur Mogge scholarships are presented to outstanding student athletes desiring to further their education at the graduate level. The Jack Tichenor Award is presented each year to the male and female student athletes in a non-revenue sport who have maintained the highest grade point average.

Financing Athletic Programs

The expense of operating the Department of Intercollegiate Athletics at Indiana University exceeds $20,000,000 annually. The program is totally self-supporting and receives no appropriated funds from the State of Indiana or the University. Operating funds are generated from ticket sales, revenue from radio and television broadcasts, revenue sharing from bowl and post-season tournaments, revenue sharing from Big Ten road games, the sale of sports merchandise, and donations from the Varsity Club. The football and men's basketball programs are IU's big revenue producers and are the only sports that operate in the black. In 1995/96, men's basketball brought in $3,767,106 from ticket sales, while football ticket sales generated $4,189,883.

The sharing of revenue in football and men's basketball is a step toward financial parity in the Big Ten. When IU plays an "away game" against a Big Ten opponent in football, the Hoosiers receive 35 percent of the host's gate receipts, capped at a maximum of $650,000 and a minimum of $250,000. Indiana receives the same percentage of the gate receipts for a basketball game played on a Big Ten opponent's court; the maximum payment is $67,000, and the minimum is $29,000.

Indiana University's athletic programs depend heavily upon the Varsity Club, a fundraising and booster organization, for much of their financial support. The club, organized in 1953, had more than 15,250 members in December of 1997. Approximately 81 percent of its members are men, 70 percent of whom are graduates of Indiana University. The Varsity Club operates in conformity with all of the rules and regulations of the NCAA and the Big Ten Conference. Regarded as a model of athletic propriety, it has been emulated by several colleges and universities. Funds generated by the Varsity Club are transferred annually to the Department of Athletics. The total for the 1996/97 fiscal year was $4,590,483.27, of which $2,811,141.77 was allocated to pay the university for tuition and fees for the student athletes. The remainder of the General Scholarship Fund of the Varsity Club was used to pay for room and board, the training table, tutoring, and textbooks. During that academic year, 262 scholarships or grants-in-aid were awarded to student athletes who qualified under the guidelines set forth by the NCAA, the Big Ten, and Indiana University—169 of these were to men (85 to football players), and 93 to women

Leanne Grotke came to IU in 1966 as an instructor in the School of HPER. She also served as director of the Women's Recreation Association, which was composed of club and intramural sports teams in which approximately 2,500 women participated each year. She served on the executive board of the AIAW and on the first board of the IWISO. She supported and helped attract coaches such as Louetta Bloecher in softball and volleyball, Kay Burrus in field hockey, Margaret Cummins in golf, Don Glass in swimming, Bea Gorton in basketball, Ann Lawver in volleyball and softball, Diane Schulz in gymnastics, and Dean Summers in tennis. She also brought Marge Albohm, one of the few certified women athletic trainers in the nation, to IU. Albohm was placed in charge of training and medical care of the women in the eight intercollegiate sports and taught in the training curriculum of the School of HPER.

(both the maximum permitted by the NCAA). A full scholarship or grant-in-aid consists of the payment of all tuition and fees for the student athlete, plus room and board.

Five levels of membership are available in the Varsity Club: for $50, one can become a Hoosier Fan; for $200, a Loyalty Fan; for $400, a Cream and Crimson Fan; for $800, a Big Red Fan; and for $2,000, a Hoosier Hundred Fan. The majority of members are in the $50 category. Varsity Club members encourage young men and women with proven athletic and scholarly ability to attend Indiana University.

Intercollegiate athletics at Indiana University have come a long way from the small sports clubs of a hundred years ago. Today's big-time college and university sports programs, particularly in football and basketball, are in the entertainment business. The top performers often compete with a view toward turning professional when their college career is over. Out of the spotlight, however, is the core group still at the heart of collegiate sports—those student athletes who compete for the love of the sport and for the glory of their school. We are proud to introduce many such athletes in the pages of this book.

Varsity Sports at Indiana University

(1883)

Baseball

Baseball was the first modern intercollegiate sport played at Indiana University. During the Civil War, baseball was a popular pastime behind the Union lines. Returned veterans who enrolled at Indiana introduced the rudiments of the sport to the campus. The first games at IU were played against intramural or town clubs in the vicinity of Bloomington. One of the team members acted as the coach/manager. Malcolm A. McDonald of Indianapolis was one of the pitchers on the 1867 team. Fifty years later, he reminisced about the sport: "There were no regulation bats, no gloves, no masks, and no pads or shields of any kind used." Of catcher Edwin C. McIntire he wrote, "McIntire displayed more grit and nerve behind the bat than anyone. He caught bare-handed, without protection of any kind, except a pair of high-topped boots with pants stuffed in at the tops. He usually took off his boots when he came to bat and ran in his sock feet. He was a corker." Allison B. Maxwell—the grandson of David Maxwell, who was the first president of the Indiana University Board of Trustees—was an infielder/pitcher/catcher on the team; he later became the first dean of the Indiana University School of Medicine.

During the early years, the pitcher stood only 55 feet from home plate (in contrast to the 60 feet 6 inches of today). Underhand pitching was the rule until 1887. A batter was entitled to four strikes (foul balls didn't count) and five balls. Batsmen called their own pitches, and a batted ball caught on the first bounce was an out.

IU's first intercollegiate game of record was played in May 1883, against Asbury College (renamed DePauw University in 1884). The Greencastle Club came down to Bloomington on the Monon Railroad. A reporter for the *Indiana Student* described the historic event: "Nine gentlemanly men from Asbury clad in neat white uniforms, met a hastily collected club of our boys on the campus, and beat them twenty-three to six.... It might be further explained that the Bloomingtons were entirely without practice, but we can say that it was a gentlemanly game, well and fairly played." The following year, Indiana defeated DePauw twice—once at Bloomington and once at Greencastle. William Julian Bryan, who later changed his middle name to Lowe after his marriage to Charlotte Lowe, played right field on the 1884 team. Bryan would later become the tenth president of Indiana University (1902–1937).

Indiana plays in the Intercollegiate Championship game against DePauw on May 30, 1892, at Seminary Field. IU won the contest 13 to 11, capping an undefeated season.

3rd Inning
Championship Game 1892.

Twelve men earned letters for their baseball play in the 1893/94 season. Eleven of them were present for this photograph: **M. D. Atwater, F. G. Ferguson, C. E. Harris, W. H. McDowell, C. W. McMullen, C. B. Malott, B. K. Myers, H. M. Scholler, C. J. Sembower, L. H. Streaker,** and team captain **C. C. Utter.** The coaches were **Berryhill** and **McIntyre. W. Mensies** was the other letter winner. Neither the number of games played nor the record of the team was recorded.

Varsity Sports at Indiana University

Following a destructive fire at Seminary Square, the campus was moved to its present location in 1885. Home games continued to be played at the University Athletic Field until 1898, when Jordan Field was put to use on the new campus. In addition to having a baseball diamond, Jordan Field was the site of a football gridiron and had a cinder track. The facility was named in honor of David Starr Jordan, IU's seventh president (1885–1891). The former playing field is occupied today by the parking lot situated immediately to the east of the Indiana Memorial Union.

A new baseball diamond constructed on Fee Lane near the end of East 13th Street became the home diamond for the Cream and Crimson in 1951. In 1960, the field was

Everett S. Dean lettered in both basketball and baseball at IU in 1919, 1920, and 1921. He was captain of the basketball team his senior year. He played center on the All–Big Ten basketball team and was the first IU basketball player to be named to the All-American first team in that sport. He was awarded the Big Ten Medal of Honor in 1921, and was later elected to the Helms Foundation Basketball Hall of Fame. Dean was offered a major league baseball contract. He turned it down because of the stigma associated with baseball in those days as a result of the Chicago Black Sox scandal.

Dean graduated from IU in 1921. After a coaching stint at Carleton College, he returned to IU in 1925 to become the head baseball and basketball coach. His baseball team won the Big Ten championship that year, and then again in 1932 and 1938. Dean also coached the Hoosier basketball teams to three Big Ten titles. He left IU in 1938 to become the basketball coach at Stanford University; his Stanford team won the NCAA title in 1942.

During his retirement, Dean served as president of the IU Alumni Association from 1957 to 1961, and as president of the "I" Men's Association in 1958. He was awarded the Distinguished Alumni Service Award in 1960. He remained active in university and civic affairs in Salem, Indiana, until his death at the age of 95 in 1993.

Coach Dean is shown here with President William Lowe Bryan, an ex–IU baseballer (1884), a staunch supporter of athletics, and a steady visitor to team practices and games.

Three thousand fans watched at Jordan Field as the Hoosiers beat Purdue by a score of 6 to 5 on June 9, 1924.

On April 1, 1925, the IU baseball team prepares to leave for a series of games in Georgia and Tennessee. Fourteen players, the senior manager, and coach Everett S. Dean (*on the far right*) made the trip. The team played Oglethorpe University, Mercer University, and Vanderbilt University, losing five games before finally defeating Vanderbilt by a score of 10 to 3.

The Big Ten season was much brighter. After defeating Purdue in the final game of the season, IU had a conference record of 10 and 3, having lost only to Chicago and Minnesota, and won the Big Ten championship, edging out Chicago, which had a record of 7 and 3. Making the trip south were outfielder and captain Sam Niness, ex-captain and catcher Earl Moomaw, pitchers Richard Woodward, Charles, and Hord, outfielders Dorsey Kite, Kaufman, Rosebruch, and Tobin, first baseman Leland Haworth, second baseman Emery Druckamiller, third baseman Davis, shortstop Hall, and reserve infielder and catcher Irwin. The team won Indiana's first Big Ten championship in baseball during Coach Dean's first season, with an overall record of 11 and 6. Kite won the Big Ten batting title with an average of .457, and seven Hoosier players batted over .300. Moomaw won the Gimbel Award, and Druckamiller was elected captain of the 1926 squad.

According to the *Indiana Daily Student,* **Whitey Wilshire** was the "ace slabsman for the Crimson diamond squad." A southpaw, he lost only 2 games while winning 17 during his short career at IU (1933–34). He had 197 strikeouts in 159 innings pitched, with an earned run average of 1.13. Wilshire joined the pitching staff of the Philadelphia Athletics under Connie Mack in 1934. He remained in professional baseball until 1938, when arm trouble forced his retirement. While playing in the major leagues, he continued his studies toward the BS degree, which he earned in 1936. He went on to earn his MS in 1939. He served as an officer at the Iowa Pre-flight School during World War II.

named in honor of Charles J. Sembower, a shortstop on the 1894 team who went on to be a professor of English and the chairman of the IU Athletic Board for many years. Sembower Field now has an underground watering system, foam rubber padding on the backstop and outfield fences, dugouts, and a broadcast booth; it has a seating capacity of 3,000 spectators.

For several years, the Hoosiers' opponents were exclusively from Indiana colleges and universities: DePauw, Butler University, Earlham College, Hanover College, the University of Notre Dame, Purdue University, and Wabash College. After IU was admitted to the Western Intercollegiate Conference (the Big Nine) in 1899, its sports teams began to compete beyond the boundaries of the state. Baseball was first scheduled as a championship sport by the Big Ten in 1896, and IU first entered Big Ten competition in 1906, when it had a record of 1 and 5 and finished seventh out of the eight teams participating.

There have been twenty-five baseball coaches at IU since the sport was introduced. The most memorable of these coaches was number eighteen, Everett S. Dean, who took over in 1924 (he was brought to IU to be the basketball coach). His baseball teams won the Big Ten

While a student at IU, **Paul "Pooch" Harrell** quarterbacked the football team and was a running back with All-American Chuck Bennett for three years (1927–29). He still holds the school record for the longest punt (86 yards), which he kicked in a game against Ohio State in 1928. Harrell was also a standout in baseball, playing third base. In the same year he kicked his record-setting punt, he led the Big Ten in batting, with a .541 average. His batting average for his entire IU career was .404, a record that has survived for nearly seven decades. After graduation, he signed a professional baseball contract with the Cincinnati Reds and spent a year with their minor league club in Akron, Ohio.

Harrell returned to IU to become the freshman football and baseball coach in 1931. In 1939 he succeeded Everett S. Dean as head baseball coach, remaining in that position through the 1947 season. During his nine-year tenure, his teams won 104 games and lost 61.

Harrell became athletic director after Bo McMillin resigned in 1948. He stepped down in 1954 because of serious health problems. While at IU, Harrell was heavily involved in improving the university's sports facilities. Following his retirement, he continued to serve as a coordinator of athletic facilities and planning.

championship in 1925 and 1932, and shared the title with Iowa in 1938. Dean left IU in 1938 to become the basketball coach at Stanford University. His successor was Paul "Pooch" Harrell, whose 1949 team shared the Big Ten title with Iowa and Michigan. Ernie Andres, who followed Harrell, coached the squad for twenty-four years. Andres-led teams finished third in the Big Ten in 1951 and 1961.

Two IU players have been named to the All-American first team: outfielder Don Ritter, in 1949, and catcher Ken St. Pierre, in 1974. Mickey Morandini is the IU career leader in runs scored (277), triples (29), and stolen bases (127); Mike Sabo is the co-leader with Mike Smith in home runs (47); Alex Smith leads in hits (305) and doubles (61). During his playing career (1927–29), Pooch Harrell posted the highest batting average, .404. Vernon "Whitey" Wilshire had the best earned run average at 1.12 during his career (1933–34).

Robert "Bob" Morgan, the present baseball coach, assumed his duties in the fall of 1983. During the five previous seasons, IU had won 95 games while losing 130. Through the 1996 season, IU had a winning percentage of 64.7 percent under Morgan's leadership—the best record

The Hoosiers take batting practice in 1937. **Bill Heldt** is the catcher, **Babe Hosler** is batting, and **Ernie Andres** is waiting his turn at bat.

of any baseball coach since the sport was introduced at IU. The Hoosiers won 57 games in 1995, and soon began making appearances in the Big Ten playoffs. In 1993, Morgan was named the Big Ten Coach of the Year. His 1996 team was the champion of the Big Ten Tournament.

Notable IU baseballers who attained some prominence in major league baseball include pitcher Vernon "Whitey" Wilshire (Philadelphia Athletics, 1934–36), third baseman Merrill "Pinky" May (Philadelphia Phillies, 1939–43), shortstop Sam Esposito (Chicago White Sox, 1952–63), first baseman Ted Kluszewski (Cincinnati

Reds, 1947–57; Pittsburgh Pirates, 1958–59; and Chicago White Sox, 1959–60), second baseman Mickey Morandini (Philadelphia Phillies, 1990–97), third baseman John Wehner (Pittsburgh Pirates, 1992–97), and third baseman Kevin Orie (Chicago Cubs, 1997). Recent standout players include shortstop Mike Smith, who won the Big Ten triple crown in 1992 with a batting average of .472, 36 RBIs, and 14 home runs; catcher Matt Braughler, who won the Big Ten batting crown in 1996 with a .444 average; and pitcher Dan Ferrell, who was named the Big Ten Athlete of the 1996 championship tourney.

Outfielder **Don Ritter** was IU's first All-American base-ball player, winning the honor in 1949. He was named to the Big Ten All-Star team as well. He had a career batting average of 351. Ritter was also an outstanding basketball player for Coach McCracken, lettering in 1947, 1948, and 1949. He was the captain of the basketball team in 1949, when IU had a record of 14 and 8. He won the Gimbel Award in 1949.

Ted Kluszewski was originally recruited to IU from Argo High School in Illinois to play football. The 6'2", 215 pounder was an All–Big Ten end, playing on Indiana's first and only unshared Big Ten championship football team in 1945. He also lettered in baseball as a first baseman and slugger. Many IU fans recall his massive clout at Jordan Field that landed on top of the Fieldhouse.

Kluszewski signed a $15,000 contract with the Cincinnati Reds in 1945. He became known for his home run–hitting ability and for his cut-off sleeves, which were necessary to accommodate his huge upper arms. Following a twelve-year stint with the Reds, he was traded to the Pittsburgh Pirates in 1957, and later to the Chicago White Sox. He and fellow Hoosier standout Sam Esposito led the Sox to the American League title in 1959. Kluszewski's home runs earned him the title of White Sox star in the World Series, although the Sox lost the Series to the L.A. Dodgers 2 to 4. Klu received the Clevenger Award in 1972.

Sam Esposito is shown here with baseball coach Ernie Andres. During his short career at IU, the multi-talented athlete was a star infielder in 1952. He also lettered in basketball that year and was a member of the football squad. Esposito spent several highly successful years with the Chicago White Sox, having signed with them for a rumored $50,000. With Ted Kluszewski, he played on the 1959 White Sox team that won the American League pennant and went on to beat the Dodgers in the World Series. He later returned to IU and earned his BS (1964) and MS (1967) degrees.

Varsity Sports at Indiana University

Ken St. Pierre, an outstanding catcher at IU, was named to the All-American baseball squad in 1974, and was also a Big Ten selection that year. He ended his career in 1974 as IU's leader in runs batted in with 83, and ranked high in doubles, triples, and home runs. St. Pierre, a solid two-sport man, was also an outstanding fullback for Coach John Pont's and Lee Corso's Big Red teams in 1971, 1972, and 1973. During his junior year he ran for 490 yards on 129 attempts and led the team in pass receptions, gaining 102 yards on 17 catches.

Alex Smith's .393 batting average during his years at IU is topped only by Paul "Pooch" Harrell's .404. Smith missed the entire 1983 season because of a knee injury. Following extensive surgery and rehabilitation, he returned to play shortstop for Coach Morgan's Hoosiers. He leads all Hoosiers with 305 hits and is tied with Mickey Morandini with 61 doubles. He is second in runs batted in, with 223, and ranks third in career home runs with 43. In 77 games in 1985, Smith hit .434 with 105 hits in 242 at bats.

Mickey Morandini was an outstanding third baseman and shortstop for IU and was an All–Big Ten selection in 1986, 1987, and 1988. He leads all other IU players with 127 stolen bases, 61 doubles (tied with Alex Smith), 29 triples, and 277 runs scored, and is second to Alex Smith with 299 hits. His collegiate career batting average was .392. Morandini was named Athlete of the the Year in 1988. He has been a successful big league second baseman with the Philadelphia Phillies.

Mike Smith was an outstanding shortstop for coach Bob Morgan. He was the Big Ten Player of the Year in 1992, when he won the triple crown: he batted .462, hit 14 home runs, and had 36 runs batted in. Following his great season, he was honored by being named the Sporting News National Player of the Year. During his four-year career at IU, Smith had 270 hits, scored 202 runs, and tied with Mike Sabo as IU's leading home run hitter, with 47 four-baggers. His .490 batting average in 1992, against all opponents, topped Ted Kluszewski's .443 in 1945. Smith was the shortstop on the All–Big Ten team in 1991 and 1992, and was named to the All-American second team in 1992.

(1887)
Football

Football was first played by Bloomington town boys as early as 1884. There is some indication that a team was organized at the IU Preparatory School soon thereafter. In 1887, Arthur Burnham Woodford, professor of political and social science, coached the IU football team in its first intercollegiate game. Woodford was a graduate of Yale University, where football had thrived since the early days of the sport. Apparently only the one formal game was played here in 1887. Indiana lost to Franklin College, 10 to 8. The squad consisted of only twelve men (the entire student body numbered only 275 that year), leaving just one man to substitute. There had been no one to practice against prior

to the contest. The football team tied DePauw in 1888, but the score was not part of the record.

Woodford resigned from his position as coach in June 1889 and returned to the East. Evans Woolen of Indianapolis took over and had coached the 1889 team for only two days when IU lost to Wabash College 40 to 2. There is no record that the team played a game in 1890. The 1891 team, coached by Joseph "Billy" Herod, played six

Pictured with the 1887 football team is **A. B. Woolford**, Indiana's first football coach, who remained at the helm until 1891.

Zora G. Clevenger was born in Randolph County, Indiana. He graduated from Muncie High School in 1900 and from IU in 1904. In 1903, he was the first "I" Man to be named to an All-American team. While at Indiana, Clevenger played at quarterback, right end, and left halfback. He won letters in both football and baseball in 1900, 1901, 1902, and 1903. In his senior year he captained both the football and baseball teams.

Cotton Berndt came to IU in 1908 from Manual High School in Indianapolis. He received his AB in economics in 1911. Berndt earned eight varsity letters while at the university: three in baseball (second base), two in basketball (forward and guard), and three in football (left end). He was captain of the basketball team in 1909, of the football team in 1910, and of the baseball team in 1911. The 1910 football team did not allow their opponents to cross the goal line all season, and their only loss was to Illinois, by a score of 0 to 3. Berndt was named to the All-Conference team his senior year.

After graduation, Berndt was named athletic director at DePauw University. He returned to IU in 1913 as the baseball coach (1913–1915) and basketball coach (1914–1915). He also served as an assistant coach in football. Following his coaching career, Berndt served as the director of welfare of the Showers Brothers Furniture Company in Bloomington from 1916 to 1935. He was a leader in the Monroe County Republican Party, serving as Bloomington's mayor from 1935 to 1939. He was safety director at IU from 1939 until his death in 1947.

games and lost five. The Louisville Athletic Club was on the schedule and was the first out-of-state rival of any IU sport.

Preston Eagleston, a halfback on the 1894 squad, was the first black member of an IU football team. He earned his AB in 1896 and his MA in 1906.

The early football games were played at the University Athletic Field in Seminary Square, but in 1898 the Jordan Field gridiron became the home of IU football. The first game played there was against Rose Polytechnic Institute, and it ended in a 6 to 6 tie. If success is measured by a winning record, the most successful IU football program was coached by Madison G. Gonterman, who came to Bloomington from Harvard; in 1896 and 1897, the IU footballers won 12, lost 3, and tied 1, for a winning

Andy Gill was an outstanding halfback and drop-kick artist in the early days of IU football. He played on the 1909, 1910, and 1911 teams, alongside such athletes as Cotton Berndt, Alice Winters, Edgar Davis, Merrill S. Davis, Homer Dutter, Allen Messick, and Ashel Cunningham. According to the *Arbutus,* Gill once played the final ten minutes of a game "with a dislocated shoulder and crushed ribs."

Jim Thorpe, the 1912 Olympic decathlon champion and an all-around outstanding athlete, was an assistant football coach at IU in 1915. He was brought in by Coach Childs to impart his knowledge and skill as a punter and drop-kicker. He is shown here with punters **Henry Grey** (*left*) and **Scott Hudson**.

Memorial Stadium was full for the Indiana–Purdue football game on November 21, 1925, the day the stadium was dedicated. The contest marked the beginning of the tradition of the Old Oaken Bucket.

percentage of 78.1. With the exception of the Louisville Athletic Club, the University of Cincinnati, and the University of Kentucky, IU's opponents consisted of local athletic clubs and Indiana colleges such as Butler, DePauw, Notre Dame, Purdue, and Rose Poly.

Slowly but surely, football began to replace baseball as the major team sport for IU and other colleges and universities. James H. Horne coached from 1898 to 1904; he is reputed to be the father of the naked reverse. IU entered Big Ten competition in 1900, compiling a record of 1–2–1 (the overall record was 4–2–2), and placing seventh in a field of nine. One of Horne's players was Zora G. Clevenger, a 140-pound halfback from Muncie who became IU's first All-American in 1903. Clevenger later served as IU's athletic director from 1923 to 1946. Coach Horne was succeeded by James S. Sheldon, whose team won eight games and lost only two in the 1905 season.

The first Homecoming celebration at Indiana, in 1909, was unplanned. It started when some students gathered after the Purdue football game to celebrate IU's 36 to 3 victory. The first planned Homecoming game was the following year, against Illinois.

The 1910 team, coached by Jimmie Sheldon, captained by A. H. "Cotton" Berndt, and featuring halfback Andy Gill, was perhaps one of the most outstanding Hoosier teams. IU's goal line was not crossed all season. The team did give up two field goals, one of which sent the Hoosiers to their only defeat (0 to 3 against Illinois), which cost them the conference championship. Berndt,

These telegrams are indicative of the urgency placed by Chicago-area Indiana and Purdue University alumni on introducing an "old oaken bucket." Athletic director Zora G. Clevenger's reply was straight to the point.

CLASS OF SERVICE	SYMBOL
TELEGRAM	
DAY LETTER	BLUE
NIGHT MESSAGE	NITE
NIGHT LETTER	N L

If none of these three symbols appears after the check (number of words) this is a telegram. Otherwise its character is indicated by the symbol appearing after the check.

WESTERN UNION
TELEGRAM

Form 1204

CLASS OF SERVICE	SYMBOL
TELEGRAM	
DAY LETTER	BLUE
NIGHT MESSAGE	NITE
NIGHT LETTER	N L

If none of these three symbols appears after the check (number of words) this is a telegram. Otherwise its character is indicated by the symbol appearing after the check

NEWCOMB CARLTON, PRESIDENT   GEORGE W. E. ATKINS, FIRST VICE-PRESIDENT

The filing time as shown in the date line on full-rate telegrams and day letters, and the time of receipt at destination as shown on all messages, is STANDARD TIME.

RECEIVED AT 75 NO V 71 BLUE

WG CHICAGO ILLINOIS 1140AM OCT 21 1925

Z G CLEVENGER

DIRECTOR OF ATHLETICS INDIANA UNIVERSITY

BLOOMINGTON INDIANA

CHICAGO ALUMNAE OF PURDUE AND INDIANA IN JOINT SESSION LAST

NIGHT DECIDED TO DONATE AND ESTABLISH AS PLAYING TROPHY AN

OLD OAKEN BUCKET WITH I OR P LINKS ADDED YEARLY AS

HANDLE WINNERS TO HAVE POSSESSION OF BUCKET GEORGE ADE

PRESENTS AT DEDICATION FOR PURDUE HARRY CURRIE FOR INDIANA STOP

MUST HAVE BUCKET IMMEDIATELY FOR ENGRAVING PLATE ETC PLEASE

SEARCH BROWN COUNTY TODAY AND SHIP TO ME IMMEDIATELY PLEASE WITHHOLD

PUBLICITY   F E BRYAN   1258PM

WESTERN UNION
TELEGRAM

Form 1207 A

CLASS OF SERVICE DESIRED	
Telegram	
Day Letter	
Night Message	
Night Letter	

Patrons should mark an X oppo-
site the class of service desired;
OTHERWISE THE MESSAGE
WILL BE TRANSMITTED AS A
FULL-RATE TELEGRAM

NEWCOMB CARLTON, PRESIDENT   GEORGE W. E. ATKINS, FIRST VICE-PRESIDENT

Receiver's No.

Check

Time Filed

Send the following message, subject to the terms
on back hereof, which are hereby agreed to

October 23, 1925.   19

To   Fred E. Bryan

Street and No. (or Telephone Number)   1216 Wrigley Building

Place   Chicago, Illinois

Have scouts trying to land oaken bucket immediately

Z. G. Clevenger.

SENDER'S ADDRESS
FOR ANSWER

SENDER'S TELE-
PHONE NUMBER

tackle Homer Dutter, guard Allen Messick, and quarterback Ashel Cunningham received All–Big Ten honors.

During the November 9, 1912, game against Iowa, IU halfback Mickey Erehart had a run from scrimmage of 98 yards, setting a Big Ten record that still stands; it was tied by Darrell Thompson of Minnesota in 1987.

In 1914, Clarence E. Childs became the new football coach, and he brought with him an assistant coach named Jim Thorpe. Neither of these two men seems to have raised IU's prowess in the sport. Ewald O. "Jumbo" Stiehm coached from 1916 to 1921, and he was succeeded by four coaches, the last of whom was Billy Hayes, prior to the arrival of Alvin C. "Bo" McMillin in 1934.

This photo, taken at halftime of the game at Harvard in 1927, is actually a composite of seven individual photographs. IU's band of 98 marching musicians, directed by Captain G. C. Cleaver, spelled out "HARVARD" while in motion. Band director Mark Hindsley placed the members in standard formation at one end of the field, and on a signal, the band formed an "H" and began to march down the field. On subsequent signals, the band formed "A," "R," "V," "A," "R," and "D."

A special train, carrying 200 people, accompanied the band and team to Boston, and the performance of the marching band earned a wildly enthusiastic ovation from the 50,000 fans in New England. Coach Pat Page's football team did not fare so well, however, losing by a score of 26 to 6. IU All-American Chuck Bennett scored Indiana's lone touchdown.

In the early twenties, a number of interested alumni urged that a stadium be built to replace the inadequate gridiron at the Jordan Field. President Bryan, a vigorous supporter of IU's athletic teams, initiated a Memorial Fund Drive to aid in this venture. Construction of the new stadium was started in 1923, in the valley northeast of the Men's Gymnasium and Fieldhouse, at the corner of Fee Lane and 10th Street. After it was completed, cracks in the concrete and other signs of deterioration appeared; IU hoped to salvage what had been done, but the construction company was uncooperative. The structure was condemned on July, 2, 1924, and was torn down. A new cornerstone was laid four months later, on November 15, the same day the last game at Jordan Field was played. IU defeated Wabash College in that contest, by a score of 21 to 7. More than 14,000 people contributed to the cost of construction of the new $250,000 stadium.

The first game on the new field was played on October 3, 1925, against Indiana State Normal College; IU won, 31 to 0. The dedication of Memorial Stadium took place on November 21, 1925. The tradition of the Old Oaken Bucket, a symbol of the football rivalry between Indiana and Purdue, was established at the ceremony. This temporary trophy would go to the winning team, which would mark the victory by adding an "I" or a "P" to the links in the chain on the bucket. The game against the Boilermakers ended in a scoreless tie, and both an "I" and a "P" were put on the chain.

The last football game at Memorial Stadium was played against the Purdue Boilermakers on November 21, 1959. Purdue won, 10 to 7. The stadium remained the site of the Little 500 bicycle race and was renamed the 10th Street Stadium in 1971. It was demolished in 1982 to make room for the Arboretum.

Construction on the fourth home of Big Red football began on August 27, 1958, near the corner of 17th and Dunn Streets. The new stadium, including development of the site and parking lot construction, cost $6,072,860. It seats 52,354 spectators. The first game on the new gridiron was played against Oregon State University on Octo-

Chuck Bennett, a graduate of Linton High School in Indiana, was an All–Big Ten back as a sophomore; was All–Big Ten, All-Western, and All-American as a junior; and captained IU's football team in 1928. He was the *Chicago Tribune*'s first Big Ten MVP and received its Silver Football. He played professionally with the Portsmouth, Ohio, Spartans and the Detroit Lions, where he was named to the All-Pro team.

Bennett returned to IU and earned the final credit for his BS degree in 1931. He went on to earn an MS in education in 1948. He taught and coached at Austin, Minnesota, and LaPorte, Indiana. From there he moved to Lyons Township High School in La Grange, Illinois, and became its athletic director. For many years he served as a recruiter of football players for IU in Chicago and its suburban area schools. In 1972, a year before his death, the "I" Men's Association presented him with the Clevenger Service Award.

The speakers' platform at the 1938 Pow Wow Banquet. From right to left: **President Emeritus Bryan, Allen G. Messick** (All–Big Ten guard in 1910 and 1911), President **Herman B Wells,** Coach **Bo McMillin,** Dean of Women **Kate Mueller,** and **Zora G. Clevenger**. Each was outfitted with the proper headdress.

ber 8, 1960. The Hoosiers lost by a score of 20 to 6.

The stadium, initially called the 17th Street Football Stadium, was dedicated on October 22, when the Michigan State Spartans defeated the Big Red 35 to 0. It was during this season that Indiana had to forfeit seven Big Ten games (all of which IU lost) as an NCAA penalty for illegal recruiting practices by supporters. Later, in 1971, the facility was named the Indiana Memorial Stadium. A 1985 remodeling of the area under the stadium added locker, training, weight, and meeting rooms, study alcoves, and two auditoriums. Light towers were later installed for use in night games. The Mellencamp Pavilion, constructed immediately north of Memorial Stadium, was dedicated on April 12, 1996. It provides a large, modern indoor practice area for the football team and for other IU sports.

Alvin C. "Bo" McMillin coached at IU from 1934 to 1947, winning 63, losing 48, and tying 11 games. His 1945 Hoosiers were the Big Ten champions, with a record of 9 wins and 1 tie. In 1967, coach John Pont's team won

IU's second Big Ten championship (shared with Minnesota and Purdue), but they lost the 1968 Rose Bowl Game to the University of Southern California. In 1979, Coach Lee Corso led IU to a Holiday Bowl victory (38 to 37) over Brigham Young. Coach Bill Mallory won two bowl games: the 1988 Liberty Bowl against South Carolina (34 to 10) and the 1991 Copper Bowl against Baylor (24 to 0). Four of his teams lost bowl games: to Florida State (13 to 27) in the 1986 All-American Bowl, to Tennessee (22 to 27) in the 1987 Peach Bowl, to Auburn (23 to 27) in the 1990 Peach Bowl, and to Virginia Tech (20 to 45) in the 1993 Independence Bowl. Through the 1997 season, IU football teams had won 172 Big Ten games while losing 370 and tying 24.

Five IU footballers (one coach and four players) have been inducted into the College Football Hall of Fame: halfback Zora Clevenger (1900–1903) in 1968; coach Bo McMillin in 1951; end and fullback Pete Pihos (1942–46) in 1966; halfback George Taliaferro (1945 and 1947–48) in 1981; and center John Tavener (1941–44) in 1990.

YOUNGEST BRAVES FOOTBALL TEAMS
Oldest Braves Special Guests

Red Team

48	Hartley	91	Marshall	29	Pletcher
25	McClintic	14	Page, E.	39	Burgess
46	Hoover	64	Johnson	36	Roman
33	Zoellers	78	Stoll	10	Bereolis
52	Alexander	80	Kennedy	28	Brennan
42	Nye	27	Comment	87	Thomas
24	Marquette	41	Merriott	61	Kimmell
93	Jakush	19	Singer	47	Waterhouse
67	Lotz	17	Bringle	32	Stebing
79	Bojinoff	11	Goffnet		

Gray Team

31	McMillan	12	Smith, Wm.	42	Smith, Ray
15	Stoshitch	75	Dobbs	73	Barrett
24	Smith, Sam	10	Katope	11	Tanner
28	Wyczawski	29	Page, J.	18	Combs
25	Hubbard	23	Benson	19	Baillie
46	Ellenwood	17	Huffman	22	Eck
47	Agenbroad	26	Lazzara	30	Rooda
33	Ruffa	39	Cooley	60	Snyder
72	Psaltis	42	Robertson	59	Weiss

Golden Anniversary of Football at Indiana

24th Annual Powwow

Sponsored by Union - A.W.S.

Men's Gymnasium

October 30, 1936

The Pow Wow Banquet became part of the Homecoming festivities in 1919. Sponsored principally by the Boosters Club, the banquet was intended to boost loyalty and enthusiasm among those who would attend the football game the following day. It was initially a stag affair; women were not admitted until 1929.

HOMECOMING WEEK-END PROGRAM

Friday, October 30

Noon	Registration of Alumni in Union Building
5:30 P.M.	Lighting the Signal Fire—Gymnasium
5:45 P.M.	Powwow—Men's Gymnasium
7:30 P.M.	Inter-Freshman Football Game in Fieldhouse
9:30 P.M.	Union-A.W.S. Dance—Alumni Hall
9:45 P.M.	I-Men Smoker in Bryan Room—Union Building

Saturday, October 31

9:30 A.M.	Law-Medic Football Game—Practice Field
11:00 A.M.	Judging of Fraternity and Sorority House Decorations
Noon	Alumni and Guests Luncheon—Union Building
2:00 P.M.	Iowa-Indiana Football Game—Memorial Stadium Between Halves—Honoring of Special Guests
4:30 P.M.	Open House—Union Building
5:30 P.M.	Phi Delta Phi Banquet—Room D, Union Building
9:00 P.M.	Band Benefit Dance—Men's Gymnasium

PROGRAM
Chief Boom Boom Dreisbach

1. Heap Big Medicine Man Zee Gee Clevenger
2. Chief Run-em-bak Jenkins
3. Princess Laughin' Water Wells
4. Chief Heap Big Chief Bryan
5. Chief U-tel-um McMillin
6. Chief Run-em-Alum Sanders

War-whoopers
Smith   Curry   Getz

Tom-tomers
I. U. Band

Sit 'em Down 'em
Pleiades and Sphinx

FEAST

A.W.S. Baked Beans

Pleiades Potato Salad

Union Cold Cuts of Meat

Aeons Halloween Fruit Cup

Sphinx Pumpkin Pie with Whipped Cream

Phi Beta Kappa Preserves

Mortar Board Rolls

Blue Key Coffee

Zora G. Clevenger is shown in 1941, seated on the right. To his right are golf coach **Hugh E. Willis** and football coach **Bo McMillin**. Standing left to right are wrestling coach **Billy Thom**, track and cross country coach **Billy Hayes**, basketball coach **Branch McCracken**, swimming coach **Robert Royer**, tennis coach **Ralph Collins**, and baseball coach **Paul Harrell**.

Upon graduation from Indiana, Clevenger became acting director of the Men's Gymnasium at IU. He coached the university's basketball team in 1905 and its baseball teams in 1905 and 1906. He then moved to Nebraska Wesleyan College, to coach football, basketball, and baseball from 1907 to 1911. He held the same positions at the University of Tennessee from 1911 to 1916 (his 1914 football team went undefeated), and at Kansas State College from 1916 to 1920, before becoming the athletic director at the University of Missouri in 1920.

Clevenger returned to IU to become the director of athletics in 1923, at which time IU had won only three Big Ten titles. He retired in 1946, after the Hoosiers won their first Big Ten football title. He came out of retirement for a few months to serve as acting athletic director when Bo McMillin left the position in 1948.

The period of Clevenger's directorship has been referred to as the "Golden Age" of IU athletics, because IU won 32 Big Ten titles, 6 NCAA championships, and 2 national AAU crowns during those years. Clevenger hired such coaches as Everett S. Dean, Billy Hayes, Billy Thom, Branch McCracken, Paul Harrell, Charlie McDaniel, Robert Royer, and Bo McMillin. In 1963, the "I" Men's Association established the Clevenger Service Award in his honor. In 1968, he was the recipient of the Distinguished Alumni Citation, and the National Football Foundation elected him to membership in its National Hall of Fame. Clevenger is widely regarded as "Indiana's Grand Old Man of Athletics."

Bo McMillin was raised in Fort Worth, Texas, and was a good friend of the Minton brothers (Sherman and Roscoe). He attended Centre College in Danville, Kentucky, where he was a member of the football team, the "Praying Colonels," when they upset the "Heralded Harvards" in the late 1910s. He was a Walter Camp All-American in 1919.

McMillin coached at Centenary College in Louisiana and Geneva College in New York prior to becoming the head football coach at Kansas State College. He came to IU in 1934, succeeding Billy Hayes, who had coached the football team for three years. McMillin won his first IU game, against Ohio University, 27 to 0, and ended the season 3 and 3, with 2 ties, after defeating Purdue 17 to 6.

McMillin called his IU teams his "pore lil' boys." He rarely turned down an invitation to speak, for fear that he might miss a good football prospect. He coached such stars as Vern Huffman, Bob Haak, John Cannady, Chris Dal Sasso, Richard C. "Corby" Davis, Frank Petrick, Russell Deal, J. C. Chestine "Rooster" Coffee (who in the early 1940s broke the ban on blacks in the old gym's swimming pool), Mel Groomes, Bill Hillenbrand, Bob Hoernschmeyer, Lou Mihajlovich, Harry "Chick" Jagade, John Tavener, Lou Saban, Ben Raimondi, Howard Brown, Pete Pihos, Ted Kluszewski, and George Taliaferro.

McMillin coached the Cream and Crimson to their first Big Ten football title in 1945, winning Coach of the Year honors. He was named athletic director in 1946. He left IU to become the coach of the Detroit Lions in 1948, and then of the Philadelphia Eagles in 1951. He left the pros because of illness and returned to Bloomington, where he died in 1952.

Anthony Thompson, a truly outstanding halfback, was an All-American in both 1988 and 1989, and was the Maxwell Award recipient and the runner-up in the Heisman Trophy voting in 1989, his senior year. Zora Clevenger was IU's first ever All-American; other, more recent first team choices have been back Vern Huffman (1936), back Corby Davis (1937), back Bill Hillenbrand (1942), end Pete Pihos (1943), center John Tavener (1944), end Bob Ravensberg (1945), back George Taliaferro (1948), back Marv Woodson (1963), back Tom Nowatzke (1964), guard Dan Croftcheck (1964), flanker Jade Butcher (1969), kicker Chris Gartner (1972), wide receiver Ernie Jones (1987), and back Vaughn Dunbar (1991).

The IU football team participates in three "trophy games": the Old Oaken Bucket game, the Bourbon Barrel game, and the Brass Spittoon game. As of the end of the 1997 season, there were 46 "P" links and 24 "I" links on the chain of the Old Oaken Bucket, as well as 3 combination links indicating ties. The Bourbon Barrel game with the University of Kentucky started in 1893, when IU tied Kentucky 24 to 24; IU leads the series 16–12–1. The Brass Spittoon series with Michigan State University, which started in 1950, is led by MSU, 33–10–1.

Football has been a source of disappointment and frustration to many IU fans, but the years have brought a few moments of pride and satisfaction. No solution to the football "problem" has yet been found. Changing coaches has been the most frequently tried remedy. Since 1887, Indiana University has had twenty-four football coaches, but only two Big Ten championships (one shared) and three post-season bowl victories, leaving many cheerless years for generations of Big Red football supporters. Coach Bill Mallory was replaced at the end of the 1996 season; in his final game, the Hoosiers retained the Old Oaken Bucket by defeating Purdue at West Lafayette by a score of 33 to 16. Malcolm G. "Cam" Cameron, a two-sport Hoosier athlete, became IU's 25th football coach, and is the first IU graduate to lead the team. His 1997 Big Red had an overall season record of 2 and 9 and went 1 and 7 in the Big Ten, defeating only eleventh-place Illinois (record 0 and 8). In the last game of the season, the Hoosiers gave up the Old Oaken Bucket after suffering their worst defeat in the history of the trophy game, 6 to 56.

Vern Huffman is the only Indiana University athlete to win All-American honors in two sports, as a center in basketball in 1935 and as a quarterback in football in 1936. He lettered in baseball in 1934. Huffman was named the Big Ten's football MVP in 1936 and won the Big Ten Medal of Honor in 1937. After earning a law degree at IU in 1940, he played professional football with the Detroit Lions. He then joined the FBI, remaining with the organization until 1945. He later returned to Bloomington and became a successful businessman and civic leader. Vern served as president of the Alumni Association in 1956 and was president of the "I" Men's Club for two years—1966 and 1977. He was one of the Clevenger Service Award recipients in 1969.

VERN HUFFMAN, QB
BIG TEN MOST-VALUABLE PLAYER-1936

Bill Hillenbrand, known as the "Evansville Express" and "Hurrying Willie," was a superb football player during his two years of play at IU. An All–Big Ten back in 1941 and 1942, he was a consensus All-American halfback, and was fifth in the Heisman Trophy balloting in 1942. He ran for 13 touchdowns in his two collegiate seasons, while passing for 18 more, and led the nation in punt returns with an average of 22 yards per return. He still leads the Big Ten in punt returns, with a total of 1,041 yards in 65 returns. He had no senior year, because of World War II, but he completed his BS requirements while stationed in Calcutta, India. He was nominated for the Sullivan Award. Bill later played professional ball with the Chicago Rockets (1946/47) and the Baltimore Colts (1947/48).

In 1990, **John Tavener** became the fourth Hoosier football player to be elected to the College Football Hall of Fame. He played at IU from 1941 to 1944. Probably the most outstanding lineman to play for Indiana, Tavener captained the team in both his junior and senior years. As a senior he was voted the team's most valuable player, and the Big Ten coaches voted him the year's outstanding lineman. He was consensus All–Big Nine and All-American that year as well.

Tavener was known as IU's "iron man." In every game, he played center on offense and tackle on defense, kicked the extra points, and called both the offensive and defensive signals.

The 1945 football team, coached by Bo McMillin, won Indiana's first and only unshared Big Ten football title. The starting lineup included **Ted Kluszewski** (83), **John Goldsberry** (78), **Howard Brown** (73), **John Cannady** (38), **Joe Sowinski** (77), **Russ Deal** (67), and **Bob Ravensberg** (61). In the backfield are **Richard Deranek** (88), **Pete Pihos** (35), **George Taliaferro** (44), and **Ben Raimondi** (40). Mel Groomes, an outstanding runner and pass receiver, frequently started instead of Deranek. 5'8", 165-pound guard Frank Ciolli started the first two games at guard against Michigan and Northwestern prior to the return of Howard Brown. Brown was voted the team's MVP. According to the roster, there were no seniors on the squad, which consisted of thirteen juniors, thirteen sophomores, and twenty-one freshmen: Goldsberry and Taliaferro were freshmen; Deranek and Kluszewski were sophomores; and Brown, Cannaday, Deal, Pihos, Raimondi, Ravensberg, and Sowinski were listed as juniors.

Hoosier back **Dick Deranek** (88) heads for the goal line behind a block by **Pete Pihos** (35) in the 1945 game against Nebraska. IU won by a score of 54 to 14. Other Hoosiers shown are **Joe Sowinski** (77), **Howard Brown** (73), and **Lou Mihajlovich** (81).

The 1945 Hoosiers are shown here having just defeated Purdue, 26 to 0, after a scoreless first half. Pete Pihos scored the first touchdown in the third quarter from the one yard line after long-gain runs by Mel Groomes and George Taliaferro, and a pass from Ben Raimondi to Taliaferro. After the kickoff, Purdue fumbled, Ted Kluszewski recovered the ball on the one yard line, and Pihos plunged for his second touchdown. In the fourth quarter, with IU up by 13, Raimondi threw a touchdown pass to Kluszewski to increase the score to 19 to 0. Raimondi intercepted a DeMoss pass, and later had a long run to the Purdue 34 yard line. He then threw a touchdown pass to sophomore reserve Lou Mihajlovich. With this win, IU captured its first Big Ten Football title, and the team added the eighth "I" to the chain of the Old Oaken Bucket. There was a push for IU to meet the heralded Cadets of Army in a post-season game. General Eisenhower denied the Cadets permission, however, saying, "The game is a good idea, but the cadets must prepare for mid-terms."

Pete Pihos, a native of Chicago, was an All-American at end and fullback and a member of the 1945 Big Ten championship team. He also played forward on the IU basketball team in 1943/44. He had a highly successful pro football career with the Philadelphia Eagles, then returned to IU as an assistant coach under Coach Smith during the spring practices of 1948 and 1949. Pihos received the Clevenger Award in 1972.

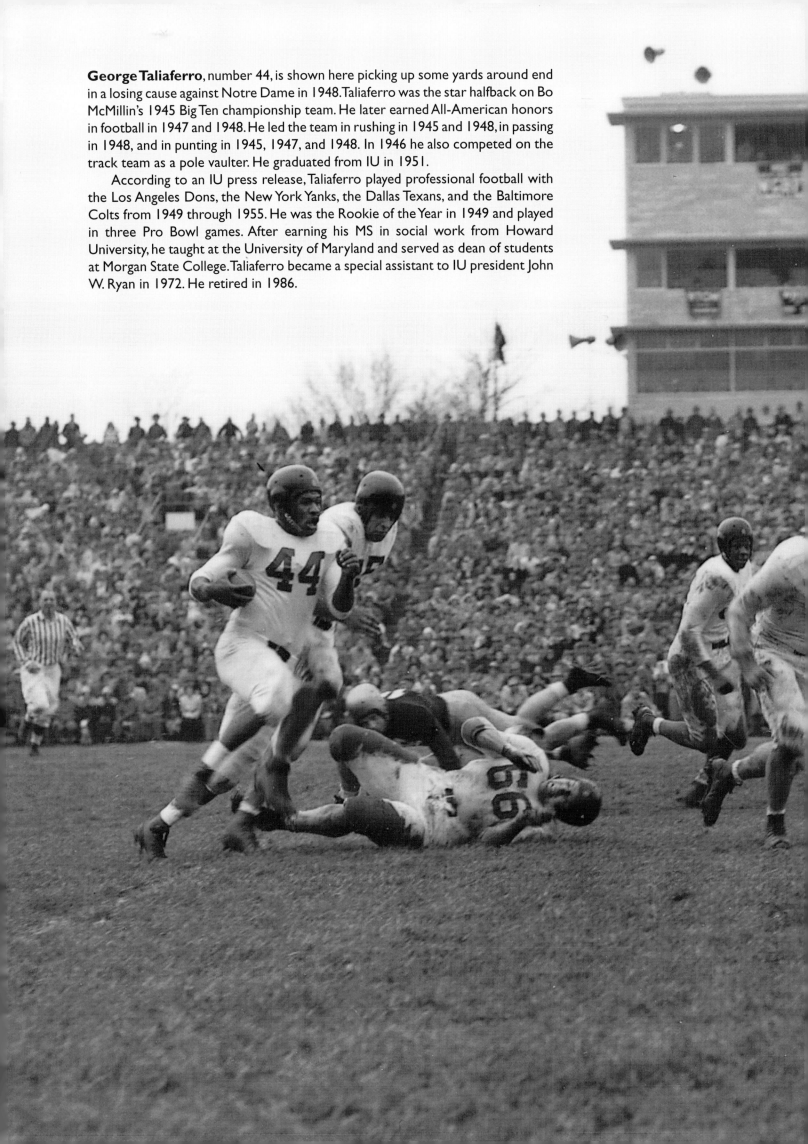

George Taliaferro, number 44, is shown here picking up some yards around end in a losing cause against Notre Dame in 1948. Taliaferro was the star halfback on Bo McMillin's 1945 Big Ten championship team. He later earned All-American honors in football in 1947 and 1948. He led the team in rushing in 1945 and 1948, in passing in 1948, and in punting in 1945, 1947, and 1948. In 1946 he also competed on the track team as a pole vaulter. He graduated from IU in 1951.

According to an IU press release, Taliaferro played professional football with the Los Angeles Dons, the New York Yanks, the Dallas Texans, and the Baltimore Colts from 1949 through 1955. He was the Rookie of the Year in 1949 and played in three Pro Bowl games. After earning his MS in social work from Howard University, he taught at the University of Maryland and served as dean of students at Morgan State College. Taliaferro became a special assistant to IU president John W. Ryan in 1972. He retired in 1986.

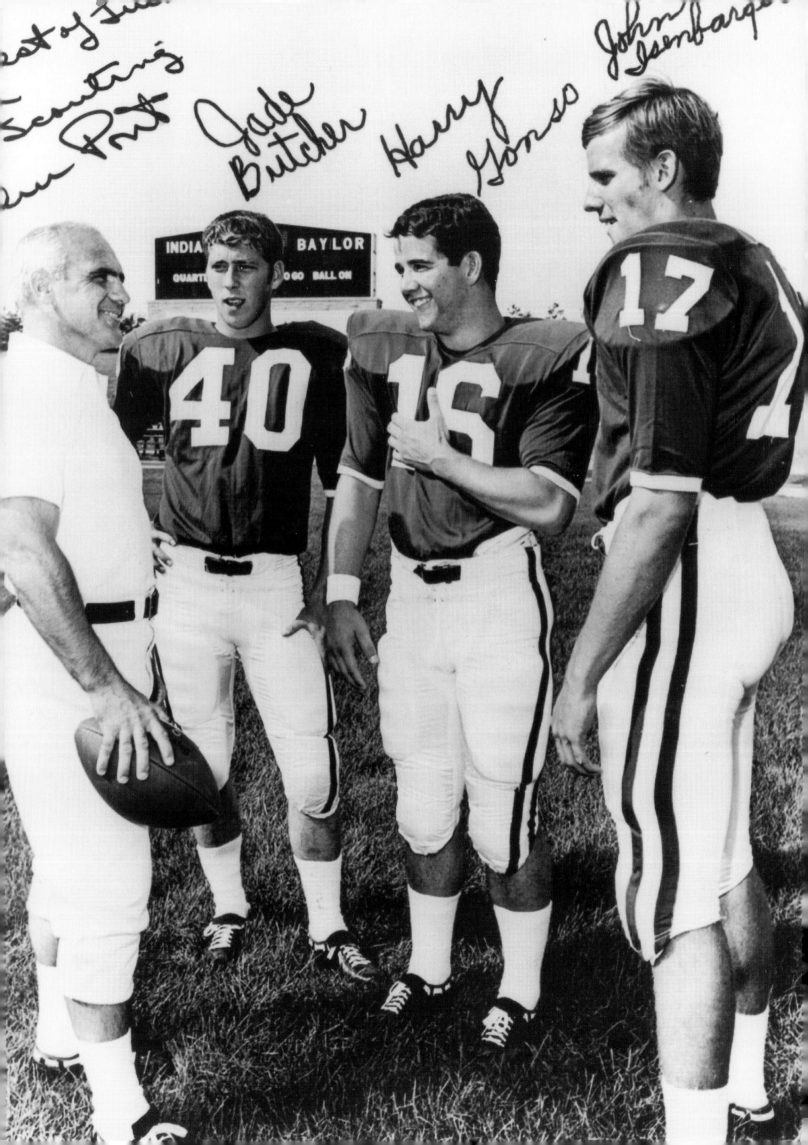

Quarterback **Harry Gonso** (number 16) moves out of the pocket in a Homecoming game against Wisconsin on November 4, 1967. Also pictured are **Terry Cole** (*left*) and linemen **Harold Mauro** (51), **Bob Russell** (64), and **Don Ghrist** (72).

Gonso rushed for 127 of IU's 198 yards in the contest and completed only 2 of 11 passes. The Hoosiers won the game by a score of 14 to 9. They had a 14 to 3 lead going into the last quarter; Wisconsin scored a touchdown but missed on the extra-point try, and the game ended with the Badgers overthrowing a pass in the end zone.

After the game, IU was ranked sixth in the nation. The Hoosiers went on to play in the Rose Bowl against Southern California.

John Pont came to Indiana as the head football coach in 1965, after leading teams to winning records at Miami University in Ohio (where he had starred as a player) and at Yale University. His 1967 Cream and Crimson squad featured such players as Harry Gonso (who later became an elected member of the IU Board of Trustees), John Isenbarger, Jade Butcher, Doug Crusan, Bill Wolff, Harold Mauro, Eric Stolberg, and Bob Russell. The team went 9 and 1 and won IU's second Big Ten championship in football, which was shared with Minnesota and Purdue. They played in IU's first and only Rose Bowl game on January 1, 1968, losing to Southern California by a score of 14 to 3. The 1967 Hoosiers were referred to as the "Cardiac Kids" because of their several come-from-behind and close wins.

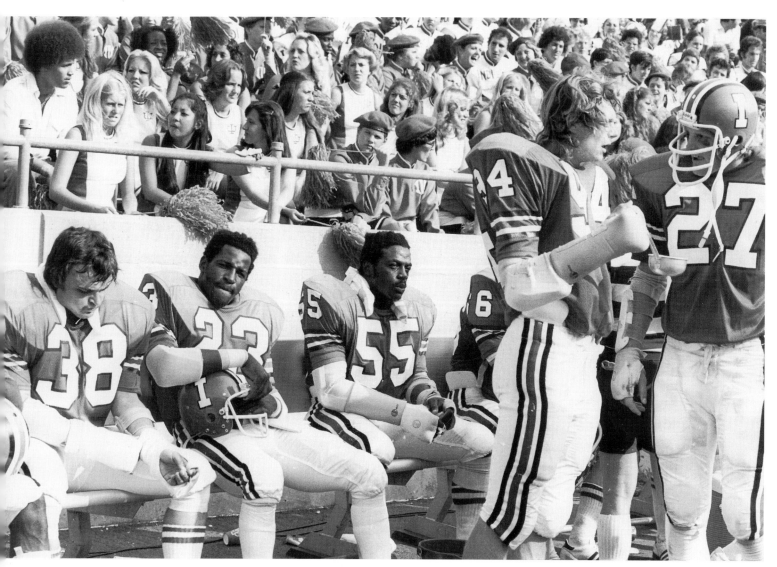

Five Indiana defensive players wait to re-enter the September 18, 1976, game against Nebraska. They are safety **Ron Hodge** (23), defensive back **Greg McIntosh** (27), linebacker **Jim Ehrensberger** (38), defensive end **Carl Smith** (53), and defensive end **George Doehla** (94).

Mike Dumas was an outstanding defensive back (safety) from 1987 to 1990. In 1990, he intercepted a pass in the Purdue game and returned the ball 99 yards for a touchdown. While at IU, Dumas set a career record of nine blocked kicks. During his senior year, he made 116 tackles. He was named the All-American safety in 1990.

At the end of the Michigan game on the chilly, rainy afternoon of October 24, 1987, a large portion of the 51,240 fans in attendance helped tear down the north goalpost. They were celebrating IU's first win against Michigan in twenty years and the first win ever against the Wolverines in Memorial Stadium. The year also marked the first time IU defeated both Michigan and Ohio State (the latter for the first time in 36 years) in a season. Coach Mallory's team had a season record of 8 and 3 and went on to play in the Peach Bowl in Atlanta.

Anthony Thompson, "A.T.," is the most honored player in the history of Indiana football. The tailback from Terre Haute set many rushing records during his college career. He leads all IU rushers with a total of 5,299 yards, and with his single-game total of 377 yards on 52 rushes against Wisconsin in 1989. Thompson scored 412 points during his IU career (1986–89), with 68 touchdowns and two 2-point conversions. He was the Big Ten Player of the Year and was only the third player in conference history to win back-to-back MVP awards, the *Chicago Tribune* Silver Football. He was All–Big Ten and All-American as a junior and senior. In 1989, Thompson won the Maxwell Award for Outstanding College Player of the Year and finished second in the Heisman Trophy balloting. He was named the Big Ten–Jesse Owens Athlete of the year in 1990. His number, 32, was retired by Coach Bill Mallory.

Thompson was a first-round draft choice of the Phoenix Cardinals. He later played for the Los Angeles Rams before retiring from professional football because of injuries. He now serves as an assistant backfield coach at IU for Coach Cam Cameron.

Vaughn Dunbar, a native of Fort Wayne, played only two seasons at IU after transferring from Northeastern Oklahoma A&M College. Here he crashes into the end zone for a TD against Kentucky in 1991. IU prevailed, 13 to 10, and went on to win the Copper Bowl. In 1991, Dunbar rushed for 1,805 yards, eclipsing Anthony Thompson's record of 1,793. He was named an All-American running back in 1991 and finished sixth in the Heisman balloting.

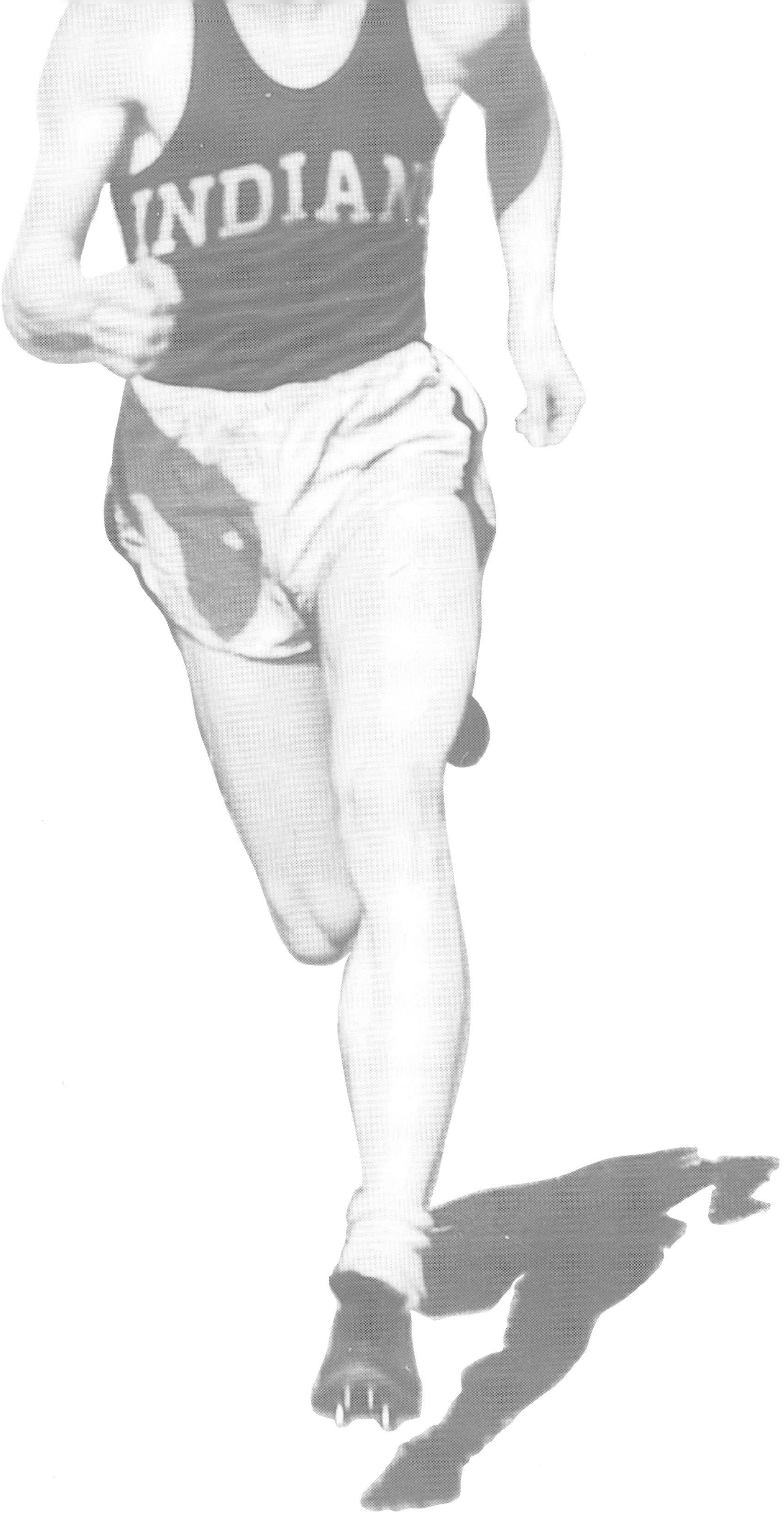
INDIAN

Men's Track and Cross Country

Indiana's first intercollegiate track and field meet was against Wabash College in 1897: it was won by IU. In 1898, under the guidance of James H. Horne, IU athletes competed in indoor meets in the new gymnasium, watched by about 500 spectators. Indiana defeated the University of Nebraska in a dual meet on May 18, 1899, and later in the month defeated Purdue. The "Hare and Hound Club" was formed on the Bloomington campus in 1901; it was the precursor of Indiana's cross country team.

Interest in track grew steadily: as the winning times decreased in the track events, the winning distances increased in the field events. The Big Ten Conference graduate directors organized and conducted the first annual outdoor track meet in Chicago in 1901, which was won by Michigan. Indiana did not take part. Indoor interclass track continued in Bloomington; in 1902, IU sent its team to compete with Purdue and Notre Dame, finishing second. The following year, the Cream and Crimson trackmen placed second to Chicago in the Amateur Athletic Union (AAU) meet held in Cincinnati. Indiana competed in its first Big Ten outdoor track meet in 1904, finishing seventh in a field of ten with 6 points. It entered its first Big Ten cross country meet in 1910, placing sixth, and its first Big Ten indoor track meet in 1915, finishing sixth in a field of eight with 0.5 points.

Outdoor track meets began to be held at the Jordan Field in 1898, then moved to Memorial Stadium on 10th Street in 1926. Beginning in 1917, indoor meets were held at the Men's Gymnasium; following the construction of the Fieldhouse in 1928, they were moved to that site.

In 1904, Indiana's Tad Shideler won the silver medal in the 120 yard high hurdles at the St. Louis Olympics. Leroy Samse placed second in the pole vault at the same Olympics; the following year, he set the world record in the pole vault at 11'5¼".

George W. Thompson, a native of Covington, Indiana, was the first black member of an IU track team. Thompson lettered in track in 1905 and 1906 and was a prominent dash man and a member of the relay teams.

The 1912 track season was considered a success, and four members of the team were almost certain to win honors at the annual Philadelphia Relays, but the Athletic Department lacked the funds to send the men.

In 1915, Clarence E. Childs, who coached both football and track, attracted wide attention to IU (and to athletics in general) when he experimented with the use of motor car–paced trials and whippet hounds in training his runners.

Before Earle C. "Billy" Hayes took over the program in 1925, there had been seven coaches in both track and cross country. Under Hayes's leadership, IU soon became one of the nation's powers in both sports. The highly successful Hayes also served a stint as Indiana's football coach, succeeding Pat Page in 1931; he was replaced by Bo McMillin in 1934.

Hayes's harriers won six straight Big Ten cross country titles, beginning in 1928 (no championships were held from 1933 to 1937). Under the tutelage of assistant coach Sid Robinson, the 1932 cross country team won the National AAU title. The team was composed of Bob Kemp, Cliff Watson, Henry Brocksmith, Charles Hornbostel, Hugh Hunter, and Pete Cuthbert. In 1936, Coach Hayes sent a six-man cross country team to participate in the National AAU meet. The team swept the events, then performed at the same level at the Central Intercollegiate Meet.

Hayes played a primary role in the organization of the NCAA Cross Country Championship Meet, the first of which was held in 1938, at Michigan State. His 1938, 1940, and 1942 teams were the NCAA champions, and one of his harriers, Fred Wilt, was the NCAA individual champion in 1942. Eight of his squads won the Big Ten team title, and seven of his runners won individual Big Ten titles: Rodney Leas, Henry Brocksmith, Dean Woolsey, Mel Trutt, Wayne Tolliver, Fred Wilt, and Earl Mitchell.

Hayes was responsible for the development of a number of elite athletes. Ivan Fuqua won an Olympic gold

Tad Shideler was one of Indiana's outstanding early track and field stars. He and Leroy Samse were IU's first Olympic medal winners. Shideler graduated from Manual High School in Indianapolis, then enrolled at IU for the spring term of 1904. In June of that year, he broke the world record in the 120 yard high hurdles at the Western Collegiate Championships in St. Louis, clocked at 15 seconds flat; the record stood until the 1920 Olympics. He was a member of the 1904 U.S. Olympic team that competed in St. Louis, where he finished second in his event, the 120 yard high hurdles. His silver medal is shown here. After his one brief but outstanding season, Shideler dropped out of school and went to work in Indianapolis.

medal as part of the 1,600 meter relay team in 1932. Don Lash set Big Ten records in the one mile and two mile events, and won the 5,000 meter run in the NCAA in 1936. In the 1948 Olympics, Roy Cochran won gold in the 400 meter hurdles and the 1,600 meter relay. Archie Harris was the NCAA discus champion in 1941 and 1942.

Coach Hayes and assistant coach Sid Robinson (a 1928 Olympic miler from Mississippi State who later became a professor of physiology at IU) were the first to investigate and use what is currently called "sports medicine." In the 1950s and 1960s, Robinson conducted extensive physiological studies on many ex–distance runners. Hayes's training methods have been termed the "Hayes Theory of Preparation for Distance Running": running over distance, followed by pace work, followed by sprinting. He believed that young athletes, in good health and condition, could absorb a great amount of hard work through the development of a proper and systematic workout schedule.

Hayes died of pneumonia in 1943. A memorial resolution read, "He had a genius for modesty and quiet achievements. Praise would embarrass him. . . . His influ-

ence for all that is good will remain one of the fine traditions of the university. . . ."

Hayes was succeeded as track and cross country coach by Cliff Watson. Gordon Fisher took over in 1945 and coached until 1962. His teams won the Big Ten cross country meet in 1946, the Big Ten outdoor title in 1950, and both the indoor and outdoor titles in 1957; Earl Mitchell, Greg Bell, Charles Peters, Milt Campbell, Bill Garrett, and Jim Roberson were some of Fisher's outstanding athletes. Jim Lavery was the coach from 1962 to 1969. The Hoosier harriers won the Big Ten meet in 1967.

Sam Bell succeeded Lavery in 1969 in both sports and has continued the winning Hoosier tradition. Bell's cross country teams won the Big Ten title in 1972, 1973, and 1980, and finished a close second in 1971 and 1979. Two of his superb harriers won Big Ten individual titles: Jim Spivey in 1980 and 1982, and Bob Kennedy in 1988, 1989, 1990, and 1992. Kennedy was Big Ten Athlete of the Year in 1990 and 1992.

Five members of Bell's team have finished in the top ten at the NCAA cross-country meet; Bob Kennedy was the individual NCAA champion in 1988 and 1992. All-

American selections were David Atkinson and Mark Gibbens in 1967, Bob Legge in 1968, Steve Kelley in 1971, Pat Madera in 1972 and 1973, Dan Hayes in 1973, Randy Stoineman in 1978, Jim Spivey in 1978, 1979, 1980, and 1982, Terry Brahm in 1982 and 1984, Scott Williams in 1987, and Bob Kennedy in 1988, 1989, 1990, and 1992. Sixty-seven of Bell's track and field athletes have been selected to the All–Big Ten first team since 1981, and Bell was named the Big Ten Track Coach of the Year in 1990 and 1992.

IU has won fifteen Big Ten indoor titles (three under Hayes and twelve under Bell) and twelve outdoor titles (two under Hayes, two under Fisher, and eight under Bell). Twenty-five Hoosiers have competed in recent Olympics, three of whom have won gold medals: Greg Bell in the long jump, Milt Campbell in the decathlon, and Sunder Nix in the 1,600 meter relay. Cream and Crimson track and field athletes have claimed six indoor NCAA titles and twenty-one outdoor titles. Kerry Zimmerman won the NCAA decathlon championship in 1983; Dave Volz and Mark Buse were outstanding pole vaulters.

An outdoor track facility was dedicated at IU on January 11, 1962, named the Earle C. "Billy" Hayes Track. The recently resurfaced facility includes a nine-lane track with a 100-foot radius on the curves. It has two shot put areas, eight pole vault areas and four pole vault runways, plus two long jump and triple jump pits with four runways. After a renovation in 1997, at a cost of $1,500,000, the facility was renamed the Robert S. Haugh Track and Field Complex. The name of the Billy Hayes Track has not been changed.

The indoor varsity track and field venue moved from the Fieldhouse on 7th Street to the 17th Street Fieldhouse in 1960. Completely renovated and modernized in 1996, this facility is one of the premier indoor facilities in the nation. It has eight 200 meter lanes for sprints and six for distance events, and includes an electronic scoring system and photo time devices. The 6,000-seat venue was named the Harry Gladstein Fieldhouse when it was rededicated in the spring of 1997.

All of Indiana's home cross country events are run on the superb course that is laid out on the University Golf Course.

Leroy Samse, a native of Kokomo, was one of IU's first Olympic medal winners, taking home the silver medal in the pole vault in 1904. He vaulted 11'9" at the state meet held in Bloomington in 1905. Samse broke the world's indoor pole vault record at 11'5½" at the Cincinnati YMCA Meet in Cincinnati in 1906. He lettered in the pole vault and the high jump at IU in 1903, 1904, and 1905.

Coach Clarence C. Childs, with encouragement from local circus impresario Frank H. Gentry, thought that the latter's circus whippets might improve the speed of IU's trackmen. There is no evidence that this proved to be true. Two unidentified IU trackmen are shown along with two whippets and their trainers.

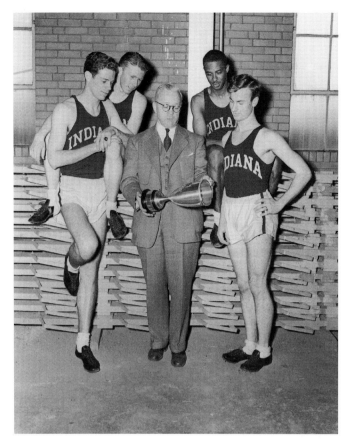

Coach Hayes admires the cup won by the track team at the Big Ten indoor track championship in 1941. **Campbell Kane**, on the left, won both the half-mile and one mile runs. Fred Wilt won the two mile; **Bob Burnett**, on Hayes's left, won the broad jump; and Roy Cochran won the 440 yard run. The team dethroned Michigan by a score of 44 to 33½. Later, IU beat out Michigan once again for the outdoor crown, 48 to 43½. Bob Burnett, Roy Cochran, Archie Harris, Campbell Kane, Marc Jenkins, Paul Kendall, Wayne Tolliver, and Fred Wilt were IU's stars. Harris and Kane each won two events and set new conference records. Cochran and Tolliver won the 440 and two mile, respectively, with Jenkins and Wilt as runners-up. Kendall finished second in the mile behind Kane, and Cochran placed second in the 220 yard low hurdles. Burnett, Cochran, Jenkins, and Kane teamed to win fourth in the mile relay. The team was undefeated in dual meets during both the indoor and outdoor seasons.

Campbell Kane was a two-time NCAA cross country champion and was key to IU's winning the NCAA title in 1940. He won the NCAA 880 yard title in 1940 and 1941. He also won the Big Ten mile and was a three-time All-American.

Fred Wilt was the NCAA two mile and cross country champion in 1941. He won the Sullivan Award (given to the nation's outstanding amateur athlete) in 1951.

Roy Cochran won the gold medal in the 400 meter hurdles at the London Olympics in 1948, setting a record, and also ran on the winning 1,600 meter U.S. relay team.

One of Coach Billy Hayes's early stars, **Ivan Fuqua** was the Big Ten champion in the 220 yard dash and 440 run in both 1933 and 1934. He broke the Big Ten half-mile record in 1934. Fuqua was a member of the U.S. 1,600 meter relay team that won a gold medal in the 1932 Olympics. He shared the Balfour Award with Charlie Hornbostel in 1933 and 1934, and won the Gimbel Award in 1934.

As a member of the IU track team, **Archie Harris** won Big Ten titles in the discus and shot put in 1940 and 1941. He was the NCAA champion in the discus throw both years. He was also an outstanding performer on the football field.

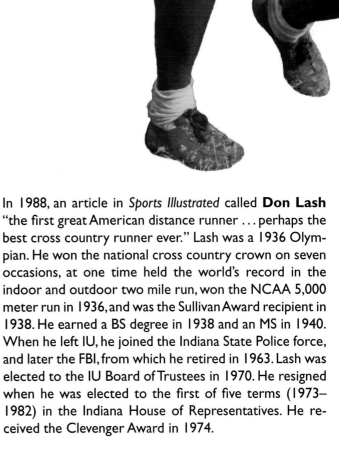

In 1988, an article in *Sports Illustrated* called **Don Lash** "the first great American distance runner ... perhaps the best cross country runner ever." Lash was a 1936 Olympian. He won the national cross country crown on seven occasions, at one time held the world's record in the indoor and outdoor two mile run, won the NCAA 5,000 meter run in 1936, and was the Sullivan Award recipient in 1938. He earned a BS degree in 1938 and an MS in 1940. When he left IU, he joined the Indiana State Police force, and later the FBI, from which he retired in 1963. Lash was elected to the IU Board of Trustees in 1970. He resigned when he was elected to the first of five terms (1973–1982) in the Indiana House of Representatives. He received the Clevenger Award in 1974.

Chuck Peters was a track star for Coach Gordon Fisher from 1948 to 1950. He was co-captain with Jim Roberson of the Big Ten championship team in 1950. He was a dash man who won Big Ten titles in the 60 yard dash in 1948 and the 100 yard dash in 1948, 1949, and 1950. His time of 21.2 seconds in the 220 yard dash in 1949 set a Big Ten record. Peters was a Clevenger Service Award winner in 1992.

IU won the 1950 Big Ten outdoor track title at the University of Illinois on April 22. The 440 yard relay (O'Brien, Garrett, Feeney, and Chuck Peters) and medley relay (Cline, Ross, DeWitte, and Owens) teams set new conference records. Bob Dellinger won the mile, and Riley finished third. Chuck Peters won the dashes, Cliff Anderson the discus, Bill Garrett the 120 low hurdles, and Jim Roberson the shot put. The mile and two mile relay teams each finished second. Co-captain Jim Roberson, who also played on the football team and earned his MD degree from IU in 1953, was one of the Clevenger Award winners in 1996. Co-captain and dash man Chuck Peters was also a winner of the Clevenger Award.

Kneeling, from left to right: **Lindy Feeney, Bill Taylor, Jack Hughes, Jim Anderson, Ed Bernauer, Charles W. Peters, Eddie Brown, Bob Kline**, and **Ken Barnes**; seated: **Bill Ross, Frank Owens**, co-captain **Jim Roberson, Jr.**, co-captain **Charles F. (Chuck) Peters, Dave DeWitte, Jack Moore**, and **Bill Linhart**; third row: assistant coach **Frank Jones, Kevin Grendley, Dave Norton, Don Anderson, Kevin Minsey, Bill Garrett, Phil Snyder, Sherman Hill**, and coach **Gordon Fisher**; top row: manager **Hoppe, Bob Dellinger, Dale View, Hal Harnet, Bob Jones, White, John Roberson, Bob O'Brien**, and manager **Grove**.

The 6'3", 210-pound **Milt Campbell**, one of the world's most versatile athletes, won the gold medal in the decathlon at the 1956 Olympic Games. His 7,937 points broke the record set by Bob Mathias at the 1952 Games, at which Campbell, still a high schooler, had placed second. While at IU, Campbell set a pair of world records in the 60 yard dash and the 120 yard hurdles. He won the NCAA 120 yard hurdles title in 1955.

Campbell was also a standout halfback at IU. In his first runback of a punt, he sprinted 77 yards for a touchdown. In addition to being an outstanding ground-gainer and pass receiver for IU, Milt was an outstanding defensive back. He went on to play professional football with the Cleveland Browns.

Greg Bell was elected to the National Track and Field Hall of Fame in 1988. Bell graduated from Garfield High School in Terre Haute in 1948. He became involved in track activities while serving in the Army in France, where he won the French Armed Forces title and the European Armed Forces title in the broad jump. He was discharged in 1953 and enrolled at IU in 1954, but he was not able to compete in track that year because of the freshman rule. Bell was the Big Ten long jump champion for three years, winning the NCAA title in that event in 1956 and 1957. With a leap of 25'8", he won the gold medal at the Melbourne Olympic Games in 1956. He also won the 100 yard dash at the Penn Relays in 1957. He was the Big Ten Medal of Honor winner in 1958. After earning his BS, Bell went on to earn a DDS at IU in 1961. He has served as director of dental services at the Logansport State Hospital for the last three decades.

Jim Spivey was the first Big Ten–Jesse Owens Athlete of the Year, in 1982. He was the Big Ten outdoor 1,500 meter champion in 1980, 1981, and 1982, and the mile and two mile titlist in 1980, 1982, and 1983. He represented the U.S. as a distance runner in the 1984, 1992, and 1996 Olympics. Spivey was also an All-American in cross country in 1978, 1979, 1980, and 1981, winning the Big Ten cross country individual title in 1980.

Sunder Nix won a gold medal at the 1984 Olympics as the lead-off runner on the 1,600 meter relay team. He won the Big Ten 440 yard run in 1981, 1982, and 1983. In 1984 he set the indoor world record in that event at the Big Ten championship meet, and also won the Big Ten 400 meter run. Nix was named the 1984 Big Ten–Jesse Owens Athlete of the Year in 1984.

Above, left: A native of Bloomington, **Dave Volz** was one of IU's premier pole vaulters. He won the Big Ten title four times, holds the IU record at 18'10¼", and is a former U.S. record holder. Volz won the NCAA pole vault title in 1981 with a vault of 17'8¼". He represented the U.S. in the 1992 Olympics, placing fifth.

Kerry Zimmerman amassed 7,810 points to win the 1983 NCAA decathlon championship in Houston. The native of Corydon, Indiana, won the Big Ten indoor long jump title in 1982 and the outdoor title in 1983. He captained the IU track and field team in 1983.

On November 29, 1936, the IU cross country team swept the National AAU championship meet, held in Newark, New Jersey. Don Lash won the event, Tom Deckard was second, James Smith was third, Mel Trutt placed fourth, and Earl Applegate was fifth, to give the IU harriers a clean sweep and a perfect score of 15 points. Harry Robbins ended the event in 23rd place. The Central Intercollegiate Meet at East Lansing, over a four mile course, also was won by IU: Lash in first place, Smith in third, Deckard in fourth, Trutt in seventh, and Applegate in eighth. From left to right: **Earl Applegate, Don Lash, James Smith, Tom Deckard, Harry Robbins,** and **Mel Trutt.**

Tom Deckard was a 1936 Olympian in the 5,000 meter run. While at IU, he teamed with Lash, Sam Miller, and Trutt to form one of the top relay teams in the nation from 1936 to 1938.

Mel Trutt was IU's only entry in the Central AAU cross country meet in 1936, and he won the event. He set the Big Ten record for the four mile run in 1938. He later coached track at Hammond High School and Drake University.

Henry Brocksmith won the Big Ten two mile run in 1930. In 1932 he repeated the victory, setting a new American record with a time of 9:13.6, then anchored the championship distance medley relay and four mile relay teams. He also won the one mile crown that year. He was awarded the Big Ten Medal of Honor in 1932. Brocksmith earned his MD degree from the School of Medicine in 1936. He was one of many distance runners at IU who came back to participate in Dr. Sid Robinson's studies on elite and older athletes.

Charlie Hornbostel won the NCAA outdoor 880 yard run three years in a row: 1932, 1933, and 1934. He broke the Big Ten indoor mile record in 1934 and was the NCAA champion in the half-mile in 1933 and 1934. He set the 600 yard record and won the mile run at the Milrose Games in 1935. He was a Clevenger awardee in 1973. Hornbostel represented the United States at the 1932 and 1936 Olympics.

Earl Mitchell is shown here with **Coach Gordon Fisher** in 1946. Mitchell won the Big Ten two mile and cross country titles in 1942 and 1946. He was a two time All-American in cross country.

Dr. Sid Robinson, professor of physiology at the IU School of Medicine and one of the world's foremost experts in the physiology of exercise, was a close colleague of Billy Hayes. For many years he tested the fitness of middle-aged and older faculty members. In the early 1960s, he began testing the physiological fitness of some of the elite distance runners, including Don Lash, Fred Wilt, Charlie Hornbostel, Mel Trutt, and Tom Deckard. He is shown here with former IU track and cross country coach and cross country runner **Cliff Watson** (*on his right*) and **Dr. Henry Brocksmith**, another early cross country runner.

1992 DIVISION I MEN'S & WOMEN'S
CROSS COUNTRY
CHAMPIONSHIPS
NCAA CHAMPIONSHIPS
INDIANA UNIVERSITY - NOVEMBER 23 - BLOOMINGTON, INDIANA

Bob Kennedy was a world-class distance runner. His father, Bob, ran on IU's 1967 Big Ten cross country championship team. The younger Kennedy won the NCAA cross country title in 1989 and 1992. He is shown here crossing the finish line in 1992, with no other runners in sight, while recording a time of 30 minutes and 15 seconds. He won the Big Ten cross country championship in 1989, 1990, 1991, and 1992.

Kennedy came to IU from Westerville, Ohio, with track as his first love. He was the Big Ten Athlete of the Year in 1990, 1991, and 1992. During his career, he won sixteen Big Ten and two NCAA track titles. In 1989, he was the Big Ten champion in the indoor mile and the outdoor 1,500 run. He retained these titles in 1990, adding the 3,000 and 5,000 meter titles. He again won all four in 1991. He was named to the All-American squad in each of his years of competition while a student at the university. He represented the United States in the 1992 and 1996 Olympics in the 5,000 meter run.

Men's Tennis (1900)

According to the 1996 *Directory of Indiana University I-Men,* J. A. Woodburn earned an "I" in tennis for six consecutive years—1884 through 1889. In 1890 a tennis association was formed at IU, and intramural matches were played on the courts of the old campus, now memorialized as Seminary Park. By 1900, the men's tennis team was competing in the state tournament at Irvington, against teams from Butler, DePauw, Earlham, and Hanover. Alvah J. Rucker and Thomas S. Harrison of Indiana won the doubles crown that year.

In 1906, three new tennis courts were opened east of Mitchell Hall; a number of players competed in an intramural tournament that spring. By 1909, the university had twelve well-kept tennis courts: four for women and eight for men. A full team was sent to the state meet at Butler that year.

From 1910 to 1933, the Big Ten team championship was awarded to the school(s) that won the singles and doubles titles. Frederick "Fritz" Bastion won the singles title for IU in 1921, and IU shared the championship with the University of Chicago. Beginning in 1934, a point system was used to determine the conference champion. The Indiana men's tennis team was not recorded as having participated in another Big Ten tennis meet until 1944, when IU finished last. Since 1965, the Big Ten champion has been determined by a combination of round-robin dual meets and a championship meet.

Indiana had had eight tennis coaches (nearly all of them uncompensated) before Dale Lewis took over the coaching duties in 1949. His teams won three consecutive Big Ten titles—in 1952, 1953, and 1954—with the 1954 team defeating Michigan by 16.5 points. John Hironimus and Bob Martin won the doubles title that year. Coach Bill Landin's team of 1964 was the most recent Big Ten tennis champion.

In 1900, **Alvah Rucker** and **T. S. Harrison** won the doubles title in the State Intercollegiate Tennis Tournament. Rucker, a transfer from DePauw, earned his AB in Greek from IU. While at Indiana, he was a star on the tennis team in both 1901 and 1902. He won letters in football in 1901, 1902, and 1903 as an end, and played left guard on the 1901 and 1902 basketball teams. He is still remembered for stealing the football in a game against Purdue in 1901, then running it back 70 yards for the game-winning touchdown.

In 1901, Rucker (*seated on the right*) and Harrison served as officers of the Indiana Tennis Association.

Fred "Fritz" Bastion brought Indiana its first Big Ten tennis championship in 1921, winning the singles title. He also won the NCAA singles title that year, beating Carl Fischer of Penn State in the championship match.

Scott Greer served as coach from 1972 until 1981, when he was replaced by Steve Greco. Ken Hydinger has been the coach since 1986; his teams have amassed a record of 193 dual meet wins, 121 losses, and 1 tie, for a winning percentage of 61.2.

On seven occasions since 1972, IU netters have been selected to the All–Big Ten team. In 1967, Dave Power won All-American honors. Other tennis standouts have included Eli Gloger, John Hironimus, Mike McLaughlin, the Salumaa brothers (Sven and Gunnar), and David McCallum. In 1995, Erik Barrett was named Big Ten Sportsman of the Year.

Indiana University is proud of its spacious and attractive tennis facilities, which permit year-round practice and play for both the men's and the highly successful women's teams. Ten outdoor courts are reserved for varsity practice and play. During inclement weather, the players move indoors to the Tennis Center, which has eight courts, locker rooms, a lounge, and seating for approximately 1,000 spectators.

Coach Bill Landin led the Hoosier tennis team to their last Big Ten title in 1964, besting second-place Michigan 69 to 48. Dave Power lost to Marty Reissen of Northwestern in the championship round in the number 1 spot. IU's number 2 man, Rod McNerney, placed third, and Charlie Kane, in the number 3 spot, placed second. Alan Graham (no. 4), Jim Binkley (no. 5), and Chill Fichter (no. 6) won their flights. Graham and Kane and Binkley and Fitcher each won their doubles rounds, while Power and McNerney lost to Reissen and Graebner in the number 1 doubles position. The team finished 13th in the NCAA championships.

Front row, left to right: **Chill Fitcher**, **Steve Erenberg**, captain **Alan Graham**, **Charlie Kane**, and **Bill Wham**; back row: coach **Bill Landin**, **James Binkley**, **Bob Wham**, **Dave Power**, **Rod McNerney**, and **Bob Scote**.

Dave Power, pictured here with coach **Bill Landin**, was a member of the 1964 Big Ten tennis championship team. A year later, he teamed with Rod McNerney to win the doubles title. Power was an All-American selection in 1967.

The 1990 men's tennis team ended the season with 19 victories and 7 losses, finishing 9 and 3 in the Big Ten. At the conference championships in Champaign, IU defeated Michigan (5–4) and Ohio State (5–2), then fell to Northwestern in the championship round. In the number 1 and 2 positions, David McCallum had an overall record of 24 wins and 19 losses, and Gunnar Salumaa was 27 and 13. In the doubles, Salumaa and David Russell won 12 and lost only 4; David Held and Tom Wiese, in the number 3 position, posted a record of 15 and 8. Salumaa was an All–Big Ten player in 1989 and 1990, and McCallum received the honor in 1990 and 1991.

First row, left to right: **Dave Held**, **Tom Wiese**, and **Mark Wittman**; second row: coach **Ken Hydinger**, trainer **John Edwards**, assistant coach **Kevin Lindley**, and assistant coach **Lars Nillson**; third row: **David Russell**, **Chris Decker**, and **Scott Mitchell**; fourth row: **David McCallum** and **Gunnar Salumaa**.

Men's Basketball

The newly constructed gymnasium, later named Assembly Hall, was 135 feet long and 66 feet wide, with a seating capacity of 1,500. It had two balconies on each side and one at the west end, and it had a bell tower on the roof. The new facility became the center for university activities and sporting events. It was the first home of the Hurrying Hoosiers basketball team. A swimming pool was added in 1909, but it was later covered by a stage. In March 1911, the gym was the site of the first state high school boys' basketball tournament, which was initiated and sponsored by the IU Booster Club. Twelve teams were invited to compete for the title. Crawfordsville High School defeated Lebanon High School in the championship game by a score of 24 to 17. The structure remained in use for student events and athletics until 1917; it was demolished in 1938.

Basketball is the only truly American sport. It originated in the United States and was not based on a game with its roots in another nation. Basketball was invented by James Naismith for a physical exercise class at the YMCA in Springfield, Massachusetts, in December of 1891. It spread rapidly throughout the East and Midwest, first through the YMCAs and then to schools and colleges. According to the *Crawfordsville Journal and Review,* "the first basketball game played outside of Massachusetts . . . was in Crawfordsville, Indiana in the Spring of 1893." It is said to have been played at the Crawfordsville YMCA. The first intercollegiate game of record was played between Yale and Pennsylvania on March 20, 1897.

The sport came to the Indiana campus in 1897, where it was played by both men's and women's teams in gymnastics classes. Intramural basketball for men soon became popular. Five games were played against other colleges in the state in 1901, beginning on February 8, when IU competed against Butler University in Irvington (Indianapolis). According to the *Indianapolis News,* "the excitement approached that of an intercollegiate football contest." Butler won that game 20 to 17, then came to Bloomington later in the month and defeated the Hoosiers again. The single game won by IU that year was against Wabash College, by a score of 26 to 17. Indiana suffered two defeats at the hands of Purdue.

During the 1902–1903 season, in addition to the usual in-state college opponents, Indiana defeated Crawfordsville Business College and Shortridge High School in Indianapolis. The next season, IU won a home game against Salem High School. The following season, the IU hoopsters went on the road, out of state, for the first time: they lost to Allegheny College in Meadville, Pennsyl-

IU played its first intercollegiate basketball game on February 8, 1901, losing to Butler at Irvington, 20 to 17. The IU box score was as follows:

	fg	ft	total
Strange	1	7	9
Unnewehr	2	0	4
Darby	1	0	2
Walker	1	0	2
Rucker	0	0	0

The team got its first win a month later, on March 8, defeating Wabash College 26 to 17 in Assembly Hall. The Hoosiers ended the season with one win and four losses, two of which were to Purdue. James H. Horne coached the team, and Ernest Strange was the captain.

Seated, left to right: **Phelps Darby**, **Ernest Strange**, **Jay Fitzgerald**, and **Alvah Rucker**. Standing: manager **Thomas Record**, **Charles Unnewehr**, **Ernest Walker**, and **Coach Horne**. E. B. Elfers was also a letter winner.

Men's Basketball

The Indiana basketball team was Big Ten co-champion in 1925/26, when the team had an 8 and 4 conference record. IU's first Big Ten title in basketball, it was shared with three other teams: Iowa, Michigan, and Purdue. IU did not play Michigan, but beat Purdue and split two games with Iowa. Art Beckner was IU's leading scorer, with 108 points; Julius Krueger had 91. Krueger was named to the All–Big Ten first team, Beckner to the second team, and Palmer Sponsler and Jack Winston to the third team. Front row, left to right: **Julius Krueger**, **Frank Sibley**, **Edward Farmer**, **Jack Winston**, **Palmer Sponsler**, **Art Beckner**, and **Bob Corell**; second row: Coach **Everett S. Dean**, **Hall** [no first name is available], **Herman Byers**, **Millard Easton**, **Harold Der**, and trainer **Jesse Fergguson**; back row: manager **George Talbot** and assistant coach **Harlan Logan**.

vania, and Hiram College in Hiram, Ohio; defeated the Rayen Athletic Club in Sharon, Pennsylvania; lost to Buchtel College in Akron, Ohio; then journeyed to Columbus, Ohio, where they lost to Ohio State.

IU's expanding sports programs necessitated that a new gymnasium be built, and on August 6, 1896, the trustees ordered its construction. The building was completed later in the year, at a cost of $12,000; it was located directly east of Owen Hall, and was called Assembly Hall.

In less than twenty years, Assembly Hall had become inadequate. In early 1915, plans were drawn up for a Men's Gymnasium; construction was approved in October. To the accompaniment of a band, President William Lowe Bryan and Dr. Burton Door Myers led a group of students on a march across the Jordan River (originally called Spanker's Branch) and up the hill from Owen Hall across 7th Street to the orchard, where the ground was cleared for the new gym. In March 1917, the 240' x 328' Tudor Gothic structure with an Indiana limestone exterior was completed at a cost of $250,000. It contained a swimming pool (30' x 90'), an indoor track, a basketball arena seating 2,400 spectators, locker rooms, offices, and a trophy room. The first basketball game was played on the new court on January 19, 1917. IU defeated the University of Iowa 12 to 7.

Soon fans seated at the ends of the court began to complain that their view was blocked by the wooden bankboards. The Nurre Mirror Plate Company of Bloomington took note of the complaints and installed 1.5-inch plate glass bankboards, referred to as "Nurre Banks." The IU basketball court most likely had the first glass bankboards in the nation.

Soon, more practice space for IU's athletes was once again deemed a necessity by the influential Hoosier alumni who backed the school's sports programs. Dr. William J. Moenkhaus, chairman of the University's Athletic Committee, submitted a proposal to the Board of Trustees to build an indoor field adjoining the Men's Gymnasium. Funds for such a structure were not available at the time, but Judge Ora L. Wildermuth, a member of the Board of Trustees, persisted in the effort. In 1926 he presented a plan for the financing of a "Fieldhouse," and his plan was pursued seriously. Plans were drawn up in May 1927, and in June the trustees approved the sale of bonds for its construction. In addition, there was a plan to levy a contingent fee of $2 per student to help with the cost.

The first game was played on the basketball court of the Fieldhouse on December 7, 1928: IU lost to DePauw by a score of 24 to 26. The facility was dedicated on December 13, 1928. That night, after a dedicatory ceremony in the Men's Gymnasium, the guests and a crowd of 8,000 fans watched the IU basketball team defeat the University of Pennsylvania, the Eastern Basketball Champion, 34 to 26. The bonds for the construction of the Fieldhouse were paid off on April 1, 1942. The last intercollegiate basketball game was played on the Fieldhouse court on February 29, 1960. Walter Bellamy, IU's All-American center, scored 24 points as the Hoosiers handed the Ohio State Buckeyes their only defeat of the year, 99 to 83. The building was named the Ora L. Wildermuth Intramural Center in 1971.

In 1960, a new Athletic Fieldhouse was constructed on 17th Street between the new Memorial Stadium and Fee Lane. In the first game played on the Hurrying Hoosiers' new home court, on December 3, 1960, 9,236 fans saw IU defeat the Indiana State Sycamores, 80 to 53. The last game was played there on March 13, 1971, when the Hoosiers lost to Illinois by a score of 103 to 87.

The current home court of the Hoosiers is Assembly Hall, originally called the University Events Stadium. It is connected to the west end of the Fieldhouse on 17th Street. Built at a cost $12,215,190, it has a seating capacity of 17,357 for basketball games. On December 1, 1971, Indiana and Ball State played the first game on the court. IU center Steve Downing grabbed 26 rebounds (still a court record) as the Hoosiers beat the Cardinals 84 to 77. Assembly Hall was dedicated and named on December 18, 1971, and its playing court was named the Branch McCracken Memorial Basketball Floor in honor of IU All-American player and coach Branch McCracken. The original floor was replaced in 1995. Assembly Hall has been filled to capacity for nearly every IU home game. It also serves as the venue for IU commencement ceremonies and other major events when the weather is inclement.

In its first twenty-eight years, IU's intercollegiate basketball program had eighteen coaches. The situation stabilized when Everett S. Dean was named the coach in October of 1924. Dean had been the first Hoosier basket-

Branch McCracken entered IU in 1926 after graduating from Monrovia High School. Although he had never participated in football before coming to IU, the 6'4", 195-pound McCracken went out for the sport, played end, and received All-American honorable mention following his first year of play. Basketball was McCracken's first love, however; he starred in each of his three years of varsity play, scoring 525 points in 51 games, and was an All–Big Ten player in 1928, 1929, and 1930. In 1930 he led the Big Ten in scoring with 147 points (a new record), was the Big Ten MVP, and was named to the All-American team. After graduation in 1930, McCracken had a brief fling with professional basketball. He then returned to IU, earning an MS in 1935. In 1966, he was a Clevenger Service Award winner. He is a member of the National Basketball Hall of Fame.

ball player to be named to an All-American first team. He served ably until 1938, winning 162 games and suffering only 93 losses before leaving to coach at Stanford University. Five of his players were selected to the All-American first team squad. Branch McCracken, another Hoosier All-American, followed Dean in 1938. His teams won two NCAA championships (1940 and 1953) and four Big Ten titles, and compiled a record of 364 wins and 174 losses through the 1965 season. Twenty-one of McCracken's hoopsters were named first team All-Americans, and McCracken himself was named National Coach of the Year in 1940 and 1953. Lou Watson followed McCracken as head coach and remained in that position until 1971.

The present coach, Robert M. "Bob" Knight, has broken all records since his arrival in 1971. His teams have won three NCAA championships (1976, 1981, and 1987) and eleven Big Ten titles. In 1974, Knight's Hoosiers won the Commissioners Conference Association (CCA) title, and on three occasions they have won the National Invitational Tournament (NIT) (1979, 1992, and 1996).

During Coach Knight's first twenty-five years at IU, his teams have produced twenty-seven first team All-Americans. Knight was named National Coach of the Year in 1975, 1978, 1987, and 1989. He was also the United States Olympic basketball coach in 1984.

Six Hoosiers have been named to the Naismith Hall of Fame: Branch McCracken (1960), Harlan Page (1962), Everett S. Dean (1966), W. R. "Clifford" Wells (1971), Bob Knight (1991), and Walter Bellamy (1993).

Branch McCracken, often referred to as "Doc," "the Big Bear," "the Sheriff," and "Big Mac," began his coaching career at Ball State Teachers College in Muncie, where he had an eight-year record of 93 victories and 41 losses. He succeeded Everett S. Dean as the basketball coach at Indiana in 1938, and replaced the fixed-play style with the fast-break or fire-engine style. His first win at IU was against Ball State (54–28). McCracken ended his coaching career at IU with 365 wins. His Hurrying Hoosiers won three Big Ten crowns, in 1953, 1954, and 1958, and shared the title in 1957. They won the NCAA championship in 1940 and 1953, defeating Kansas both times. McCracken was named National Coach of the Year in 1940 and 1953, and was later inducted into the Helms Foundation Basketball Hall of Fame as a coach.

McCracken coached such players as John Wallace, Ralph Hamilton, Don Ritter, Lou Watson, Bill Garrett, Sammy Miranda, Ernie Andres, Don Schlundt, Bobby Leonard, the Van Arsdale brothers (Tom and Dick), Tom Bolyard, Jon McGlothlin, and Jimmie Rayl. He retired as coach in 1965 but remained on the faculty as a professor of HPER. After his death in 1970, one of his players said, "Coach McCracken will always be an inspiration to me, because he was young enough to appreciate me, humble enough to know me, creative enough to inspire me, aggressive enough to challenge me, inspirational enough to stimulate me, and, most important, his moral characteristics served as a model for my life."

With a season record of 17 and 3, Coach McCracken's 1939/40 basketball team was selected to play in the eight-team NCAA tournament. IU defeated Springfield College in the opening game 48 to 24, then downed Duquesne 39 to 30 to advance to the finals against Kansas. The Hurrying Hoosiers had a 13-point lead at halftime and went on to defeat Kansas by a score of 60 to 42. Indiana shot 34 percent in the game, considered phenomenal at that time. Marv Huffman was voted the MVP of the tourney, and Jay McCreary and Bill Menke made the All-Tournament team.

Front row: **Jim Gridley**, **Herm Schaefer**, **Bob Dro**, team captain **Marv Huffman**, **Jay McCreary**, **Paul Armstrong**, and **Ralph Dorsey**; back row: **Coach McCracken**, **Chet Francis**, **Bill Menke**, **Andy Zimmer**, **Bob Menke**, and manager **Ralph Graham**.

Nine of the eleven members of the 1939/40 team, plus Coach McCracken, have been elected to the Indiana Basketball Hall of Fame in New Castle. At the 40th reunion of the team in 1980, Governor Otis R. Bowen conferred the honor of Sagamore of the Wabash on each of the living members.

Paul "Curly" Armstrong played professional basketball for several years with the Fort Wayne Zollner Pistons. Ralph Dorsey was a basketball coach and athletic director in Horse Cave, Kentucky. Bob Dro, a native of Berne, Indiana, became field secretary of the IU Alumni Association in 1948, and later served as an administrator in the Department of Athletics. Chet Francis was basketball coach of the Vincennes Alices and a bank president. Jim Gridley, a native of Vevay, Indiana, was a basketball coach at Charlestown, Indiana. After earning his MS in 1954, he became the athletic director and basketball, baseball, and track coach at Rushville High School. Marv Huffman earned his BS degree in business and took a job with the Goodyear Tire and Rubber Company. While working in Akron, Ohio, he played basketball with the Goodyear team in the National Professional League for a year.

Lawrence "Jay" McCreary, who had played on the Frankfort High School championship team in 1936, went on to be the head coach at Muncie Central High School. His Muncie Central Bearcats won the IHSSA title in 1952; his 1954 team was defeated in the finals by Bobby Plump and Milan High School. McCreary also served as head coach at LSU for eight years.

Bill Menke, a member of the U.S. Naval Air Corps, was killed in a flying accident near San Juan, Puerto Rico, in World War II. His brother, Bob, returned to Huntingburg, Indiana, after the war and earned a master's degree. He has run a highly successful furniture-manufacturing business, and was elected to two terms on the Indiana University Board of Trustees. Herm Schaefer played professional basketball with the old Minneapolis Lakers. He later coached the Indianapolis Olympians. He was a regional manager for the Ford Motor Company. Andy Zimmer captained the basketball team in 1942 and won both the Balfour and Gimbel awards. After earning his BS in education, he went on to a career in the Marine Corps, advancing to the rank of lieutenant colonel.

Receiving the 1969 Clevenger Service Award along with **Vern Huffman** were **Dr. Merrill S. Davis** and **Donald C. "Danny" Danielson**. Davis won three letters in basketball and captained the team in his senior year. He also earned letters for his play on the 1910, 1911, and 1912 football teams. He was a member of the Booster Club that organized the first Indiana State High School Basketball Tournament for boys. Davis earned his MD degree from IU in 1914, and became the first president of the School of Medicine Alumni Association. He served as president of the IU Alumni Association and was a member of the Indiana University Board of Trustees for six years.

Danielson was an outstanding baseball player, earning letters for his play during the 1939, 1940, and 1941 seasons. He was head coach of the baseball team in 1948. He was the assistant alumni secretary for two years. He was a member of the Indiana University Board of Trustees for twenty-one years and served as its president from 1969 to 1980.

John Wallace (10), one of IU's leading scorers during his three years of play (1945–1947), goes up for a rebound in a 1946 game against Minnesota. Number 40 is **Robert Mehl**; the other IU player in the photo is **Norbert Herrmann**.

Bill Garrett, number 8, is shown here taking a shot against Illinois. Garrett led the Shelbyville High School basketball team to the Indiana high school state championship in 1947. When some IU alumni from Indianapolis told President Herman B Wells that this young African American would like the opportunity to play basketball for Indiana University, Wells responded that Garrett could certainly become an IU student, but whether he played basketball would be up to Coach McCracken. Garrett did come to IU, where he broke the Big Ten basketball color line.

The 6'2" Garrett played center for the Hoosiers for three years (1949–51), leading the team in both scoring and rebounds each year. He was one of the smoothest pivot men in IU history. At the end of his three years of play, he led all Hoosiers in career points (792), and his 193 points in 1951 were the most scored by an IU player in a single season. The 1951 Hoosiers were 19 and 3 and ranked very high in the wire service polls. Garrett, who was also known as "Bones" because of his skinny physique, was named IU's MVP, and earned All-Conference and All-American honors. In addition to playing basketball, he was a member of the track team, winning the Big Ten 120 yard hurdle title and competing on two winning relay teams in 1950.

Upon graduation, Garrett was drafted by the Boston Celtics, but for financial reasons he played for the Harlem Globetrotters. He served in the Army during the Korean War, then resumed play for the Globetrotters. He coached the 1959 Crispus Attucks High School basketball team to the state championship, and was assistant dean for student affairs at IU–PU/Indianapolis. He died in 1972, at the age of 45, following a heart attack. His son William said, "He had the right temperament to break the color barrier. He was aggressive, but not confrontational. Every time I see a documentary about Jackie Robinson, I notice his character attributes are similar to those of my father."

Varsity Sports at Indiana University

The Indiana University basketball team won their second NCAA championship under Branch McCracken in 1953. The starting five consisted of **Charlie Kraak** (13), **Dick Farley** (31), **Don Schlundt** (34), **Burke Scott** (25), and **Bobby Leonard** (21). Schlundt led all scorers with 661 points, followed by Leonard with 424; the two were All–Big Ten selections.

McCracken's 1954 Hoosiers seemed destined to repeat their Big Ten and NCAA championships. The starting five returned, and four highly capable subs were available: Phil Byers, Paul Poff, Dick White, and 7' center Lou Scott. The Hoosiers won the Big Ten title and advanced to the sixteen-team NCAA tournament, but they lost their first-round game to Notre Dame by a score of 65 to 64.

Overleaf: McCracken's team, captained by Bobby Leonard, won the Big Ten with a 17 and 1 record, losing only to Minnesota (83–65). IU was rated number one in every poll. In the NCAA Tournament, the Hoosiers downed DePaul, Notre Dame, and Louisiana State to earn a place in the finals. The team again defeated Kansas, the defending champions, but this time in a very close game, by a score of 69 to 68. Center Don Schlundt led IU in scoring with 30 points. Charlie Kraak chipped in with 17, and Bobby Leonard's free throw with twenty-seven seconds remaining on the clock clinched the victory. Both Schlundt and Leonard won All-Tourney honors.

The Hoosiers are shown here celebrating their NCAA victory and receiving awards. Kneeling, left to right: **Dick Farley**, **Phil Byers**, **Burke Scott**, **Dick White**, and **Don Schlundt**. Standing: freshman coach **Joe Thomas**, **Jim DeaKyne**, assistant coach **Ernie Andres**, **Goethe Chambers**, **Bobby Leonard**, **Branch McCracken**, **Charlie Kraak**, **Jackie Wright**, **Paul Poff**, **Jim Schooley**, and manager **Ron Fifer**.

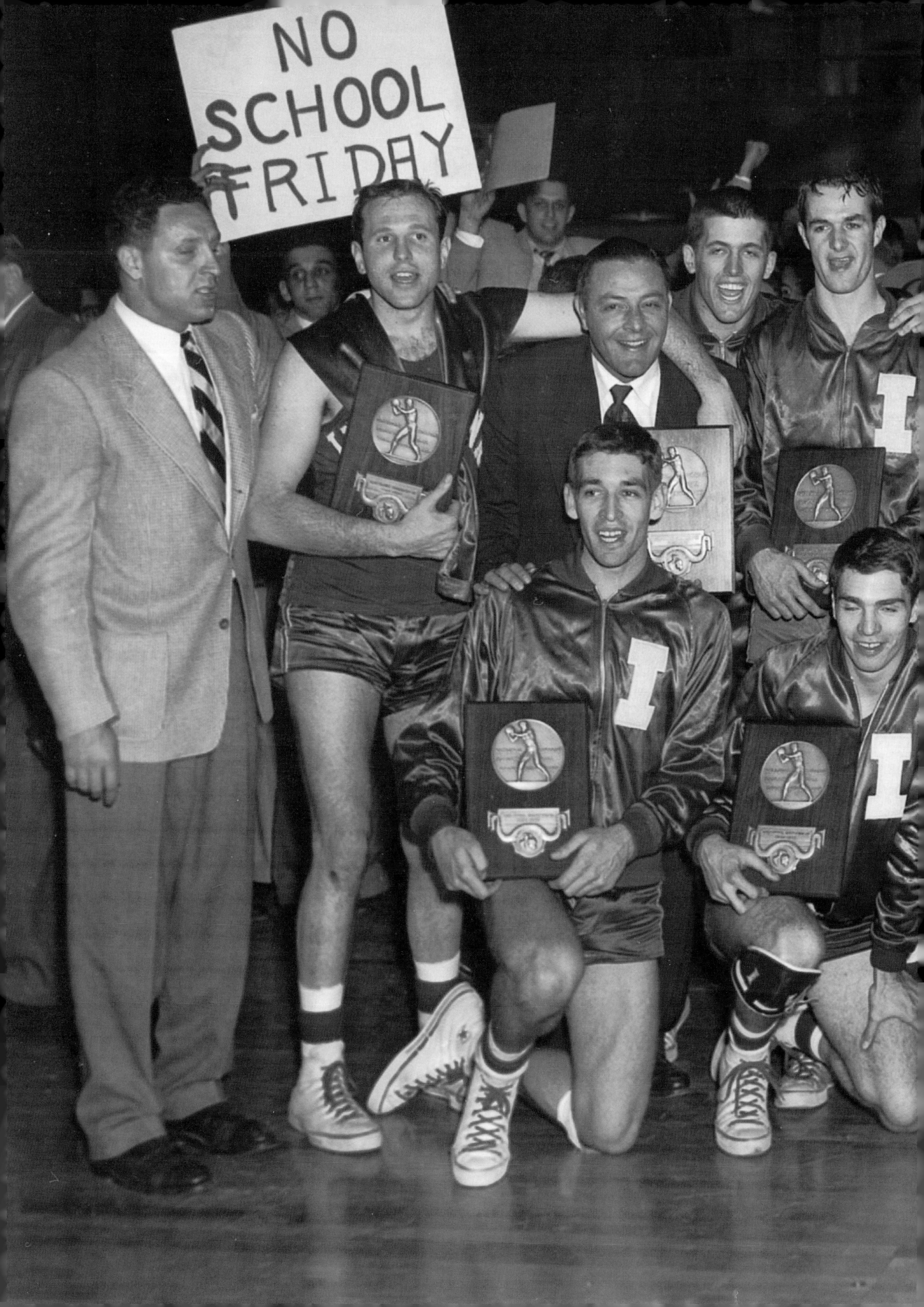
NO SCHOOL FRIDAY

Don Schlundt, number 34, is shown here taking a shot against DePaul in one of the 1953 NCAA Tourney games. The star center was one of the Big Ten's first quick and agile "big men" in the early 1950s. He led the Hurrying Hoosiers to their second NCAA title in basketball in 1953. Schlundt received the Clevenger Award in 1980.

One of Branch McCracken's star players on the 1953 NCAA basketball championship team, **Bobby Leonard**, number 21, is shown here taking a one-handed shot against DePaul. An excellent long-range shooter, Leonard later played professional ball with the Indiana Pacers of the American Basketball Association. He was the Pacers' coach for many years, and later the color man on their radio and television broadcasts.

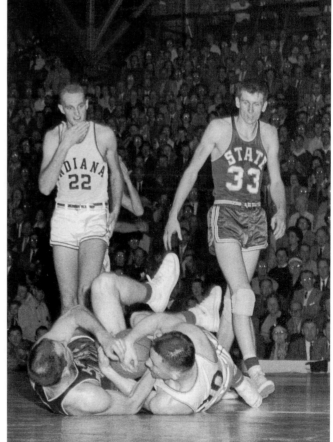

Archie Dees, number 22, watches a fight for the ball in a game against Michigan State, with IU leading 57 to 50. Archie was the Big Ten MVP in both 1957 and 1958 and was selected to the All-American team as a center both years. He ranks 13th in scoring at IU, with 1,546 points during his three-year career. His season average in 1958 was 25.5 points. Dees won the Balfour Award in 1958.

Sophomore **Jimmie Rayl**, number 22, is shown here taking one of his patented shots in a game against Ohio State on February 20, 1961, in the first season of play in the 17th Street Fieldhouse. Also pictured are IU players **Dave Porter** (43), **Gordon Mickey** (30), and **Ernie Wilhoit** (on the right), and OSU players **Jerry Lucas** (11), **Larry Seigfried** (21), **John Havlicek** (5), and **Robert "Bobby" Knight** (24). One of Coach McCracken's leading scorers, Rayl earned All-American honors, but he scored only 2 points in the loss (69 to 73) to OSU. On two occasions he scored 56 points: against Minnesota in 1962, when he made 20 out of 39 shots, and against Michigan State in 1963, when he took 48 shots and hit 23. He scored 1,401 points during his three-year career as a Hoosier.

Overleaf: **George McGinnis** played only one season with the Hurrying Hoosiers, 1970/71. He was named to the All-American and All–Big Ten teams and was IU's MVP. He scored 719 points, with an average of 29.9 points per game, a record that still stands. The number one draft pick of the Indianapolis Pacers of the ABA, he played ten years in the ABA and NBA.

Men's Basketball

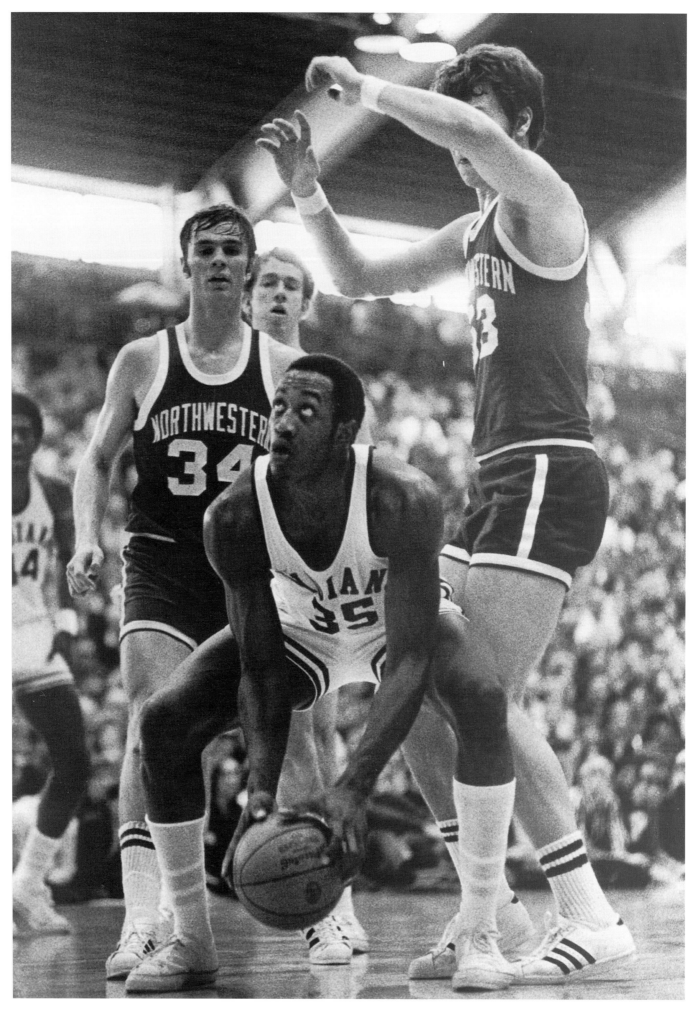

Varsity Sports at Indiana University

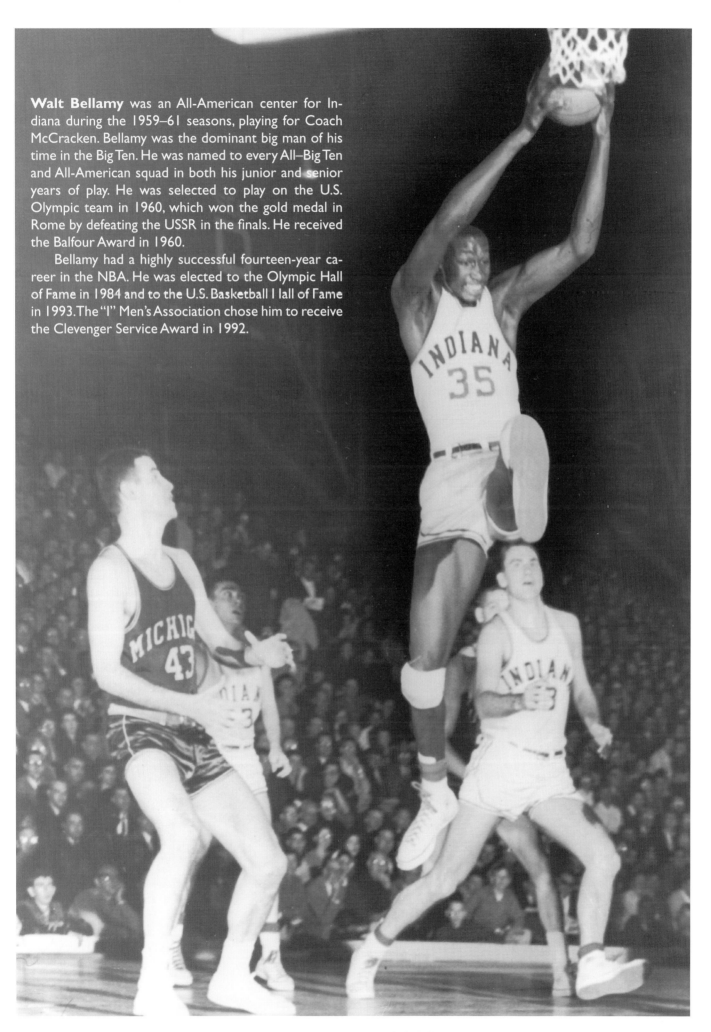

Walt Bellamy was an All-American center for Indiana during the 1959–61 seasons, playing for Coach McCracken. Bellamy was the dominant big man of his time in the Big Ten. He was named to every All–Big Ten and All-American squad in both his junior and senior years of play. He was selected to play on the U.S. Olympic team in 1960, which won the gold medal in Rome by defeating the USSR in the finals. He received the Balfour Award in 1960.

Bellamy had a highly successful fourteen-year career in the NBA. He was elected to the Olympic Hall of Fame in 1984 and to the U.S. Basketball Hall of Fame in 1993. The "I" Men's Association chose him to receive the Clevenger Service Award in 1992.

Steve Downing was an outstanding shot-blocker and rebounder during his IU career (1971–1973). He was an All-American and All–Big Ten player and the Big Ten's MVP in 1973. He was the number one pick of the Boston Celtics and played on their 1974 NBA championship team. He has served as an associate director of athletics at IU since 1979.

Steve Green was one of Bob Knight's earliest recruits and turned out to be one of the leading contributors to Coach Knight's early teams. The 1975 Big Ten championship team, which Green captained, was undefeated in the regular season, but lost to Kentucky (90 to 92) in the NCAA regional finals. Green was an All-American in 1974 and 1975. He was a first-round draft pick by Utah, and played in the pros with St. Louis and Indiana until 1979. He later returned to IU and earned his DDS degree in 1984. He now practices dentistry in Indianapolis.

John Laskowski is shown here receiving instructions from Coach Knight prior to entering a game. Laskowski was known as "Super Sub," although he also received many starting assignments. He played on the 1973, 1974, and 1975 Big Ten champion basketball teams. Laz is now the marketing director for the Indiana University Alumni Association. He and Ted Kitchel are the broadcast team for the Hoosiers' basketball games on television.

The 1975/76 Hoosiers take to the floor in the pre-season intrasquad game. The Cream were led by Kent Benson, and the Crimson by Scott May. Those identified are, from left to right: **Kent Benson, Quinn Buckner, Jim Wisman, Rick Valavicius, Tom Abernethy, Bob Bender, Scott Eells, Jim Crews,** and **Scott May**.

The previous year's team, which had included Steve Green and John Laskowski in addition to all of the 1976 starters, had been undefeated going into the NCAA Tournament, but they lost in the regionals to Kentucky after Scott May broke his wrist. The 1975/76 team made up for that disappointment: they finished the season 32 and 0, emerging from the NCAA Tournament as the national champions.

Indiana defeated St. John's, Alabama, Marquette, and UCLA in tournament play before meeting Big Ten rival Michigan in the title game. The Hoosiers trailed by six points at the intermission, after losing Bob Wilkerson to a concussion early in the contest. They rallied in the second half, however, and went on to defeat the Wolverines 86 to 68, to claim Coach Knight's first and IU's third NCAA title. May and Benson led the scoring with 26 and 25 points, respectively; Buckner added 16, and Abernethy chipped in for 11. Benson was named the tourney's MVP, and he, May, and Abernethy made the All-Tournament team.

Photo copyright © by Dave Repp.

Scott May, with **Kent Benson** blocking out, is shown here taking a jump shot against Notre Dame. May was a major contributor to IU's third NCAA basketball championship, in 1976. His injury the year before had brought an end to what was shaping up to be an undefeated season. May was voted the 1976 College Player of the Year and was a member of the winning U.S. Olympic basketball team. He was the number one draft pick of the Chicago Bulls that year. His NBA career ended after six years because of knee injuries. He went on to play six more years in the Italian league.

When Indiana University recruited the 6'3", 205-pound **Quinn Buckner** in 1972, it acquired a leader and a superb athlete. Many considered Buckner to be the top high school athlete in the nation in 1971/72. He had led Thornridge High School of Dalton, Illinois, to two consecutive state basketball championships. He was an outstanding defensive back in football for coach Lee Corso for two years, but later channeled his abilities solely into basketball. He is shown here bringing the ball downcourt against Michigan State.

Buckner leads all Hoosiers with 542 career assists. He was the captain of the team that won the gold medal at the World University Games in Moscow in 1973. He led the Hoosiers to four Big Ten championships—1973, 1974, 1975, and 1976—as well as to a CCA crown in 1974. The team had a heartbreaking near-miss in the 1975 NCAA Tourney; but they came back to win the national championship in 1976. That same year, Buckner captained the U.S. Olympic basketball team to a gold medal.

Buckner played in the NBA with the Milwaukee Bucks, the Boston Celtics, and the Indiana Pacers. He helped lead the Celtics to an NBA title in 1984. (Thus he had been a member of a championship basketball team at every level of play—from high school through the pros.) He later served as a TV sports commentator for CBS, leaving to coach the Dallas Mavericks of the NBA during the 1993/94 season. He has since returned to his former role in TV.

Mike Woodson is shown here at halftime of a 1980 football game after accepting the *Chicago Tribune* Award as the 1980 Big Ten MVP in basketball. Woodson won four letters in basketball (1977, 1978, 1979, and 1980). He served as team captain in 1979 and as co-captain in 1980. He was a Helms Foundation All-American in 1979. Early in the 1979/80 season, Woodson sustained a back injury, and on December 27, 1979, he underwent surgery to repair a herniated disc. Seven weeks later, in his first game back, he scored 18 points against Iowa and had three rebounds and five assists. He led the Hoosiers to a Big Ten title that season and was named the Big Ten's MVP. He stands fourth in career scoring at IU with 2,061 points. Woodson was the number one pick of the New York Knicks, and spent thirteen years in the NBA. He is now an assistant coach for the Milwaukee Bucks.

The 1981 Hoosiers won IU's fourth NCAA basketball championship, the second under Coach Knight. The team also won the Big Ten, with a record of 14 and 4. **Ray Tolbert**, named the conference MVP, shows off the NCAA championship emblem. The starting five of Ted Kitchel, Isiah Thomas, Ray Tolbert, Landon Turner, and Randy Wittman led the Hoosiers in every statistic. Also adding to the team's success were Steve Bouchie, Tony Brown, Chuck Franz, Glen Grunwald, Phil Isenbarger, Steve Risley, and Jim Thomas.

On their march through the NCAA Tournament, the Hoosiers defeated Maryland (99 to 64), Alabama-Birmingham (87 to 72), St. Joseph's (78 to 46), and Louisiana State (67 to 49). In the title game, after leading by one point at the half, they pulled away to defeat North Carolina by a score of 63 to 50. Isiah Thomas scored 23 points in the game; Randy Wittman added 16, while Landon Turner hit for 12. Isiah Thomas was named the tourney's MVP, and he, Turner, and Jim Thomas were named to the All-Tournament team.

This would be junior Landon Turner's last basketball game. On July 25, 1981, he was injured in an automobile accident that left his lower extremities paralyzed. Turner had been named Player of the Game in the NCAA games against both St. Joseph's and LSU. He was elected team captain for the 1982 season. He was drafted by the Boston Celtics in 1982, and the United States National Broadcasters Association made him an honorary member of their 1982 All-American Team. Turner returned to the university and earned his bachelor's degree in 1984.

Men's Basketball

Isiah Thomas (11), alongside **Ray Tolbert** (45), is shown here rebounding against Iowa. **Steve Bouchie** is on the far left. Thomas, who spent only two years at IU, led all scorers in 1981, his sophomore season, with 545 points, followed by Tolbert with 428. Tolbert led the team in rebounds with 224; Thomas led in assists with 197, and had 74 steals in 34 games. Thomas was named to the All-American team that year. He chose to forgo his remaining eligibility and entered the NBA draft. (He later completed the requirements for his degree in forensic studies.)

The 19-year-old sophomore was selected by the Detroit Pistons and played thirteen years as a pro. He was on the NBA All-Star team twelve times, and led the Pistons to two NBA championships. After retiring from pro ball in 1994, he served as vice president of the Toronto Raptors of the NBA. He resigned from that position in 1997 to become a TV broadcaster.

Dan Ferrell was an outstanding southpaw pitcher during his career at IU (1994–1996). He helped lead the Hoosiers to the 1996 Big Ten championship, and was named the tournament's most valuable player.

INDIANA vs. WISCONSIN

Dads' Day

- OCTOBER 7, 1961
- INDIANA UNIVERSITY STADIUM
- OFFICIAL PROGRAM
- FIFTY CENTS

CAPT. BILL OLSAVSKY

Official Program • Twenty-F...

ANA vs TEXAS CHRIST...

...ol Day

MEMC...

...2 P.M. • ...

50

Many themes have been featured on the covers of IU's football programs. The 1931 program was in memory of Notre Dame coach Knute Rockne. The 1933 Boy Scout Day edition introduced the new coach, Bo McMillin. The 1949 High School Day program emphasized the non-players of the game, while the 1961 Dad's Day program celebrated the problems of a "dad."

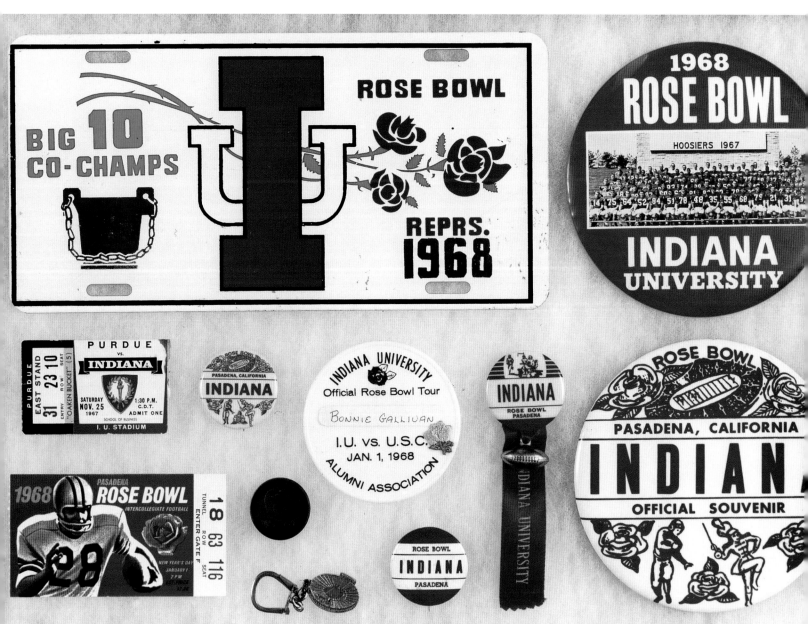

Indiana's participation in the 1968 Rose Bowl led to the introduction of badges and a license plate for loyal fans and alums. Ticket stubs from the Purdue game and the Rose Bowl game are shown here. USC defeated the Big Red by a score of 14 to 3. From the Collection of John Pfeifer.

Always a supporter of IU athletics as well as academics, Chancellor **Herman B Wells** enjoys a good view at a 1983 football game.

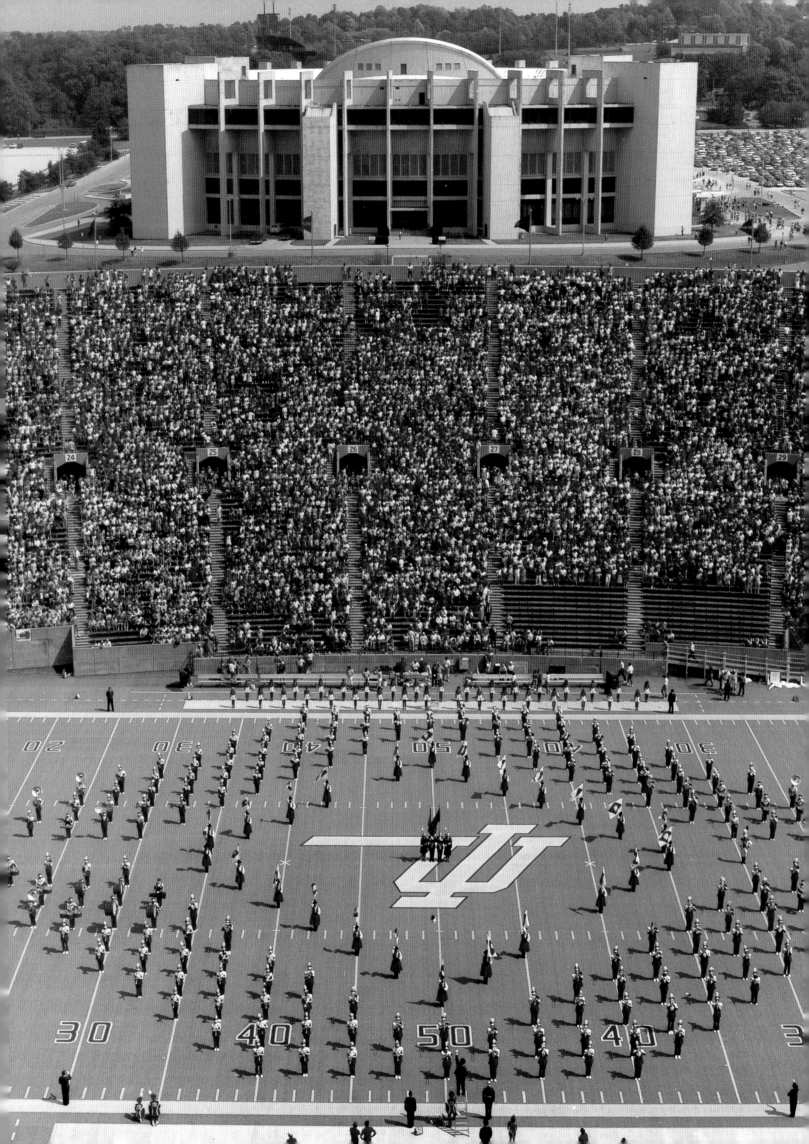

Special events accompany every college football game, both before the contest starts and at halftime. Here the Hoosier Hundred go through their musical paces; the pep band plays; band director Wilbur England follows the tradition of turning hats backwards following a victory; the flag girls perform; the cheerleaders lead the yells and éxecute their stunts; the Red Steppers perform their routines; a baton twirler twirls; and a loyal fan proclaims that IU is Number 1.

Big Red quarterback **Steve Bradley** prepares to launch a pass in the 1983 game against Michigan State. IU won the contest, 24 to 12.

Bill Mallory served as Indiana's head football coach from 1984 through 1996. He had coached previously at Miami of Ohio, Colorado, and Northern Illinois. After a poor first season, his IU teams took on a winning tradition. Mallory's Hoosiers were invited to play in five post-season games: the 1986 All-American Bowl, the 1987 Peach Bowl, the 1988 Liberty Bowl, the 1990 Peach Bowl, and the 1991 Copper Bowl. Following his last victory as the coach at IU—an Old Oaken Bucket win (33 to 16) over Purdue at West Lafayette on November 23, 1996—he was carried off the field by his players.

Thomas Lewis, one of IU's leading punt and kickoff returners, is shown here receiving a punt. The wide receiver leads all Big Red receivers with 148 receptions during his career (1991–1993). In the 1993 game against Penn State, he caught 12 passes and gained 285 yards.

Alex Smith charges around end in a 1994 game. In his three years of play for IU, he rushed for 3,492 yards, a total second only to Anthony Thompson's. He had ten games in which he rushed for more than 150 yards. His longest gain from scrimmage was an 81-yard run against Southern Mississippi in 1995.

Trent Jones takes a punt return in for a touchdown in the first quarter of the 1996 game against Iowa. Following Bill Manolopoulos's extra-point kick, IU led by a score of 7 to 0. Iowa went on to win, however, by a score of 31 to 10.

A native of Nebraska, **Sam Bell** was already a successful coach before coming to IU. His cross country team at Oregon State won the NCAA crown in 1961. Bell became IU's head track and field and cross country coach in 1969, and has maintained one of the nation's top programs in both of these sports. His Hoosiers dominated the Big Ten in 1973 and 1974, winning the triple crown by bringing home the championships in cross country and both indoor and outdoor track. Bell was selected to coach the men's distance runners for the U.S. Olympic team in 1976. He coached the winning World Cup team for the U.S. in 1979.

Mark Buse, a graduate of Southridge High School in Dubois County, Indiana, was a six-time All-American pole vaulter. He set the Big Ten indoor record in the vault in 1994 at 18'6¾", surpassing the record set by former IU vaulter Dave Volz. He won the NCAA title in 1993. During the 1993/94 season, Buse won the Big Ten and Penn Relays. He received the Balfour Award in 1995.

Nathan Davis was one of Indiana's top two-sport athletes. As a defensive end in football, he was one of the Cream and Crimson's leading tacklers and won honorable mention in the Big Ten. He was drafted by the Atlanta Falcons in 1997. In track and field, he was one of the nation's top shot put and discus throwers, placing third in the NCAA shot put in 1995 and winning All-American honors. Davis won the Gimbel Award for track and field in 1997.

In 1995, **Erik Barrett** was the Big Ten Sportsman of the Year and an All–Big Ten tennis team member. He is currently enrolled in the Indiana University School of Medicine.

Coach **Bob Knight** is shown here addressing the crowd at Assembly Hall after the last game of the 1995 basketball season. Knight played on the great Ohio State teams of the early sixties. His first collegiate coaching job was at the United States Military Academy at West Point, where he raised the Army Cadet teams to a new level of respectability. He became IU's head coach in 1971. Knight introduced a tenacious man-to-man defense and superb passing and screening offense to Big Ten and national play. His highly successful style has been emulated by many college coaches in the U.S.

Knight's teams have won three NCAA titles, three NIT titles, one CCA title, and eleven Big Ten championships (two of which were shared). He coached the U.S. team to the Pan American title in 1979 and to the Olympic championship in 1984 at Los Angeles. He has coached more than a dozen All-Americans. His many outstanding players have included Steve Downing, Joby Wright, Steve Green, John Laskowski, Tom Abernethy, Kent Benson, Quinn Buckner, Scott May, Jim Crews, Bob Wilkerson, Mike Woodson, Ray Tolbert, Landon Turner, Isiah Thomas, Ted Kitchel, Randy Wittman, Steve Alford, Keith Smart, Uwe Blab, Eric Anderson, Greg Graham, Damon Bailey, Alan Henderson, and Brian Evans. His teams have been invited to participate in twenty-one NCAA tournaments, and they have been in the Final Four on six occasions.

As Coach Knight returns to the bench, the Hoosiers take the floor after a time-out in the final game of the Indiana Classic against Illinois State in 1983. The IU players are **Stew Robinson** (22), **Chuck Franz** (23), **Marty Simmons** (50), **Steve Alford** (12), and **Uwe Blab** (33). Indiana won the game by a score of 54 to 44.

Rick Calloway (20), **Stew Robinson** (22), **Daryl Thomas** (24), and **Andre Harris** wait for a rebound in a 1986 game against the University of Illinois. The Hoosiers defeated the Fighting Illini, 71 to 69.

The Hoosiers clinch the 1987 NCAA Championship at the Louisiana Superdome in New Orleans on a last-second shot by **Keith Smart** (23; on the far right). **Joe Hillman** (44), **Dean Garrett** (22), **Daryl Thomas** (24), and **Steve Alford** wait for the rebound that never came. The final score was Indiana 74, Syracuse 73.

Calbert Cheaney was the Big Ten MVP in basketball in 1993 and was awarded the *Chicago Tribune* Silver Basketball. Here he shows off the NIT pre-season championship trophy won by the team in 1992. In 1993, Cheaney was a consensus All-American and the Collegiate Player of the Year. He leads all IU scorers with 2,468 points. He won the Balfour Award in 1992 and 1993. Cheaney was selected in the first round of the 1993 NBA draft by the Washington Wizards. He is currently one of the team's leading players.

Damon Bailey drives past an Ohio University player in an NCAA Tourney game in 1994 at Landover, Maryland. IU won the game by a score of 84 to 72. The Hoosiers were bumped out of the tournament two games later by Boston College.

Bailey played at Indiana alongside teammates such as Matt Nover, Todd Leary, Eric Anderson, Calbert Cheaney, Alan Henderson, Greg Graham, Pat Graham, and Brian Evans. In each of his years at IU, the Hoosiers played in the NCAA Tournament; in 1992 they made it to the Final Four. During his college career, Bailey scored 1,741 points and had 474 assists and 132 steals.

Alan Henderson, who played basketball for IU from 1992 to 1995, ranks fifth in scoring with 1,979 points and first in rebounds with 1,091. In this 1994 photo, he pushes back a rebound for 2 points against Illinois.

Left-hander **Brian Evans** was named the Big Ten's most valuable basketball player in 1996. During his last year of play with the Hoosiers, he led the team in scoring, rebounding, and field goal and free throw percentage. In his four-year career at IU, Evans hit 186 3-point field goals, to lead all Hoosiers. He was drafted by the Orlando Magic as a first-round NBA pick.

Considered by some (including his coach, Duane Goldman) to be one of IU's best wrestlers, **Roger Chandler** won his second Big Ten title at 142 pounds in 1997, finishing second in the NCAA. The previous year he had finished third in the NCAA. Chandler served as the team's captain for two years. He had 134 wins (the most by any IU wrestler) during his college career, suffering only 25 losses. He leads all Indiana wrestlers with 40 pins. Chandler was named IU's Athlete of the Year in 1997.

IU's six NCAA swimming championship banners are on display at the Counsilman Pool.

Big Ten swimmers wait for the starting gun at the annual conference swim championships at the Counsilman Pool in 1997.

Randy Leen, a native of Ohio, where he won the state title in 1993, is probably one of IU's finest golfers. In the summer of 1996 he had the lowest score, 291 (three shots better than Tiger Woods), of any amateur in the U.S. Open. He was named Big Ten Golfer of the Year in both 1996 and 1997, and was the Big Ten tourney runner-up in 1997. Leen defeated teammate Don Pagett III in the quarter-finals of the National Amateur Tourney before being defeated in the semifinals of medal play. In 1998 he was ranked among the top ten amateurs in the U.S.

Randy Wittman played on the 1981 NCAA championship team. He was the Big Ten's Most Valuable Player and an All-American in 1983. Wittman, number 24, is shown here with **Steve Bouchie** (54) in a game against Ball State. Wittman was a first-round draft pick by the Atlanta Hawks and played in the NBA for eight years. He is currently an assistant coach for the Minnesota Timberwolves of the NBA.

Ted Kitchel was a member of the 1981 NCAA basketball championship team, and was named to the All-American team in 1982 and 1983. He was IU's MVP in 1982. Kitchel scored 1,336 points during his career (1980–1983), and led the team in 1982 with 568 points. He leads all Hoosiers in 3-point field goal shooting with his 0.656 percentage in 1983. In a game against Illinois in 1981, Kitchel made 18 out of 18 free throws. He has the third-highest Indiana free throw percentage.

Captains **Steve Alford** (12), **Daryl Thomas** (24), and **Todd Meier** led the 1987 Hurrying Hoosiers to a conference record of 15 and 3 and an overall record of 30 and 4. The team won the Indiana Classic, the Hoosier Classic, and the Big Ten, then went on to take the NCAA championship in New Orleans. Here they show off the NCAA championship plaque.

The Hoosiers started NCAA play by defeating Fairfield (92 to 58). They then downed Auburn (102 to 90), Duke (88 to 82), Louisiana State (77 to 76), and Nevada–Las Vegas (97 to 93) before meeting Syracuse in the finals. IU won the game 74 to 73 on Keith Smart's last-second shot from the corner baseline. Alford, Rick Calloway, Dean Garrett, and Smart led the scoring, while Garrett and Calloway led the rebounding throughout the six games of tournament play. The team had a strong bench, including Steve Eyl, Tony Freeman, Joe Hillman, Todd Jadlow, Dave Minor, Jeff Oliphant, Magnus Pelkowski, Brian Sloan, and Kreigh Smith.

Steve Alford, shown here driving around a Syracuse player in the championship game of the 1987 NCAA Tournament in New Orleans, led the 1987 Hurrying Hoosiers to their fifth NCAA championship in basketball, hitting seven 3-point shots in the final game. Steve learned the game of basketball under the watchful eye of his father, high school basketball coach Sam Alford, in New Castle, Indiana. He was a member of the gold medal–winning U.S. Olympic basketball team in 1984. In his senior year of play he earned the Big Ten–Jesse Owens MVP award, and he was a consensus pick for the All-American first team basketball squad. Steve's achievements at IU include the Big Ten record in free-throw percentage, a shooting percentage of 0.530 at 3-point range, and the individual game scoring record, 42 points, at Assembly Hall. He received the Big Ten Medal of Honor and the Big Ten Athlete of the Year award in 1986 and 1987.

Alford was selected in the second round of the NBA draft by the Dallas Mavericks. He spent two years in Dallas, plus one year with the Golden State Warriors. After his stint in the NBA, he became a successful college basketball coach. He is currently the head coach of the University of Iowa.

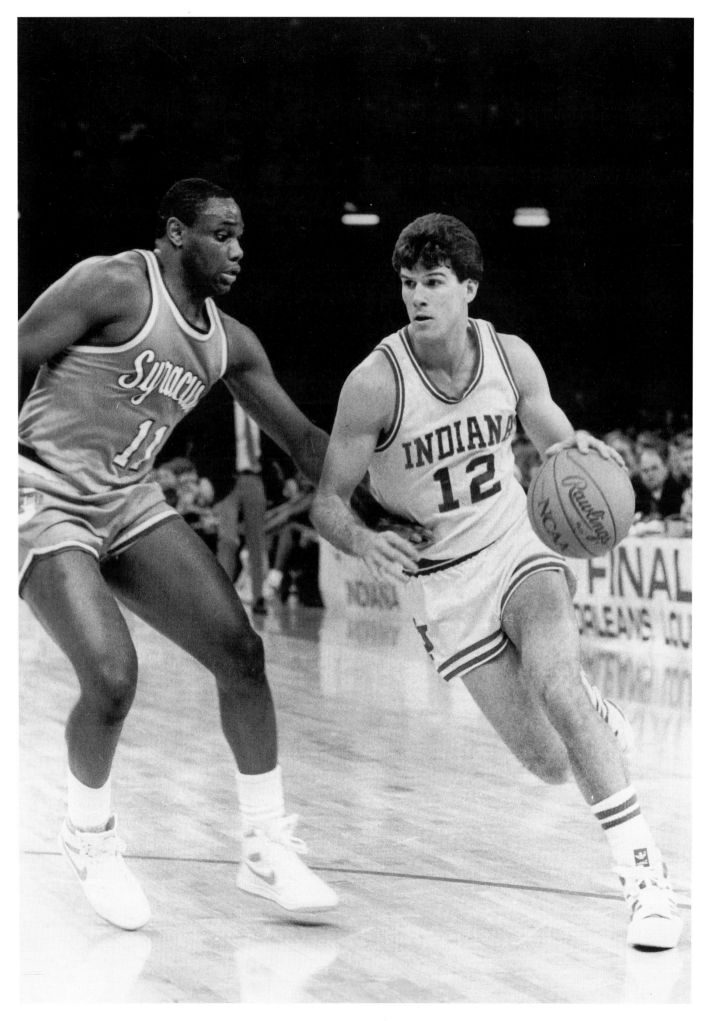

(1911)

Wrestling

The first "I" awarded to an Indiana wrestler was earned by Walter B. Bodenhafer in 1911. The sport began to grow under coach Elmer E. Jones (1910–1914), whose 1914 grapplers won the Big Ten championship, Indiana's first-ever Big Ten title. Jones was succeeded as coach by Edgar C. "Big Ed" Davis, an outstanding athlete during his college career at IU who earned ten letters in three sports: four in wrestling (team captain in 1913 and 1914), three in football (team captain in 1914), and three in track. James Kase led the Hoosiers to their second Big Ten title in 1921, and Jack Reynolds's 1924 and 1925 teams shared the Big Ten title with Illinois.

William H. "Billy" Thom, a professional wrestler, became the coach in 1927. During his eighteen years at the head of the program, he brought national prominence to the school. He taught IU's wrestlers how to use their legs as well as their upper body in wrestling. His 1932 team won the NCAA title, and several of his players won individual NCAA and Big Ten titles. He was named coach of the 1936 U.S. Olympic wrestling team, and three of his wrestlers were on the team. He also served as the line coach of Bo McMillin's 1945 Big Ten football champions.

Thom's teams won 110, lost 21, and tied 3 dual meets. They won eight Big Ten wrestling titles during his tenure: 1931, 1932, 1933, 1934, 1936, 1939, 1940, and 1943. Charlie McDaniel, who had won two NCAA heavyweight titles under Coach Thom, succeeded him as coach in 1946 and remained in that position until 1971. Fourteen of McDaniel's wrestlers won Big Ten titles, and twelve were voted All-American honors. Overall, his teams won 147 dual meets, lost 138, and tied 11. In 1973 the team was taken over by 1968 Olympic champion Doug Blubaugh. Blubaugh had been voted

A native of Salem, Indiana, **Ed Davis** was a three-sport athlete at IU, competing in wrestling, football, and track and field. He was the heavyweight champion on the 1914 wrestling team, which brought home IU's first ever Big Ten title. Davis coached the IU grapplers in 1915 and 1916. He later played with Knute Rockne and Jim Thorpe in the early days of professional football. He earned his MD degree at IU in 1919 and practiced medicine as an eye, ear, and nose surgeon in Muncie. He was one of the Clevenger Service Award winners in 1964.

Below: **Charlie McDaniel**, a 1933 graduate of Bloomington High School, wrestled for IU under coach Billy Thom, compiling a record of 41 victories and only 5 losses. In 1936 he was the NCAA heavyweight champion and was selected to a berth on the U.S. Olympic squad. He captained the IU team in 1938, when he went undefeated with 15 wins. He won both the Big Ten and the NCAA heavyweight crowns that year. He was also an outstanding tackle on the football team, winning All–Big Ten honors and honorable mention on the All-American squad. He was the Big Ten Medal of Honor winner in 1938.

McDaniel taught and coached at several Indiana high schools before returning to IU to coach in 1945. He led the IU wrestlers for twenty-seven years, compiling a record of 145 wins, 139 losses, and 11 ties, and producing twelve Big Ten champions. During most of this time he also served as the chief football scout. He was selected to the Helms Athletic Foundation's Wrestling Hall of Fame in 1966.

Above: **William H. "Billy" Thom**, a veteran of World War I, earned his BS degree from the State University of Iowa in 1923. He played on Iowa's Big Ten championship football team in 1922, and also lettered in track and wrestling. He served as athletic director and coach of all sports at Wabash High School in Wabash, Indiana, before becoming Indiana's head varsity wrestling coach and head freshman football coach in 1927. In 1929 he became the assistant (line) varsity football coach.

Thom was a colorful and highly respected personality in wrestling circles at the national, state, and university level. His Hoosier wrestlers won eight Big Ten and two NCAA titles. His dual meet record at IU was 105 wins, 25 losses, and 4 ties. He was named coach of the 1936 U.S. Olympic wrestling team. Three of his wrestlers were on the team: Willard Duffy, who wrestled at 123 pounds; Dick Voliva, at 174 pounds; and Charles McDaniel, at 191 pounds. Voliva, who had been a Big Ten titlist and NCAA winner, brought home a silver medal.

While serving as coach at IU, Thom maintained an active career in professional wrestling. He captured the world middleweight title in 1928 and retained it until 1937, when he retired as undefeated champion. He estimated that he participated in about 500 bouts in Indianapolis alone, and more than 2,500 bouts by the time he resigned from his coaching job at Indiana in 1945. After a short sojourn in California, Thom returned to Indianapolis as a sports promoter. In 1955, he was appointed by Governor George Craig to be the state athletic and recreational director of state institutions.

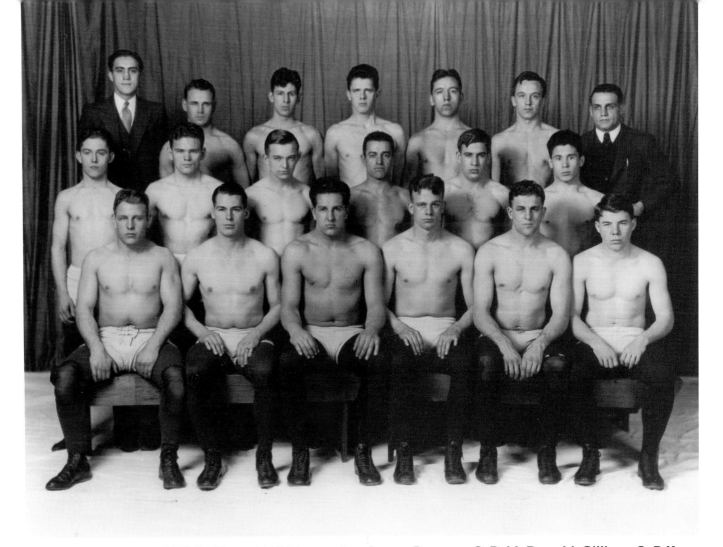

The Hoosiers were the 1932 Big Ten and NCAA wrestling champs. First row: **C. D. McDonald**, **Gilliam**, **O. P. Kuss**, **R. I. Jones**, **A. H. Rascher**, and **Richard Voliva**; second row: **D. E. Aldridge**, **C. B. Hawkins**, **Bush**, **Fox**, **Brown**, and **Cellini**; third row: manager **M. J. Sugar**, **D. A. Goings**, **Scott**, **P. H. Devine**, **G. H. Belshaw**, **Ed P. Belshaw**, and coach **Billy Thom**.

At the NCAA meet, held in Bloomington on March 25 and 26, Ed Belshaw won the 134-pound crown, Goings placed second in the 145-pound class, and Rascher and Jones placed third in their divisions—174 and 191 pounds, respectively. IU nosed out Oklahoma A&M College by 3 points (14 to 11).

The Hoosier grapplers also won the Big Ten wrestling championship, held in Bloomington. Ed Belshaw, D. A. Goings, and George Belshaw won the 135-, 145-, and 155-pound titles, respectively. R. I. Jones retained his heavyweight crown, while Aldrich (118 pounds), Hawkins (126 pounds), and McDonald (175 pounds) were runners-up. Richard Voliva placed third in the 165-pound class that year. In 1934 the Bloomington native was the NCAA and Big Ten champion at 175 pounds, and in 1936 he won an Olympic silver medal.

the Outstanding Wrestler in the World in 1960. Over the next eleven years, his teams compiled a record of 106 wins, 138 losses, and 7 ties. He was followed by Jim Humphrey (1985–1989) and Joe McFarland, whose teams had a combined record of 66 wins, 71 losses, and 1 tie.

The current coach, Duane Goldman, a four-time All-American wrestler from the University of Iowa, has coached the Hoosiers since 1993. His wrestlers have won 34 dual meets while losing 20 and tying 1.

IU grapplers have won thirty-six individual Big Ten crowns, beginning with Ed Davis at heavyweight in 1914. Championships have been captured at all weight levels: Robert Myers won the 118-pound title in 1936 and 1937; Mike Rolak won at 121 pounds in 1946; Willard Duffey was the 126-pound champion in 1936 and 1938; Pat

Devine won in the 135-pound class in 1933 and 1934; Brian Dolph was the 150-pound titlist in 1989 and 1990; Richard Voliva was the 175-pound champion in 1934; Bob Jones was the heavyweight champion in 1932 and 1933, while Charlie McDaniel won that title in 1938. Eight IU wrestlers have won NCAA crowns. The most recent IU wrestlers to earn All-American honors were Brian Dolph, in 1988, 1989, and 1990; Jess Lyons, who wrestled at 142 pounds in 1990 and 1992; Chris Russo at 126 pounds and Scott Priche at 150 pounds, in 1994; and Roger Chandler, a 142-pounder, who was honored in 1995. Brian Dolph, NCAA champion in 1990, had a winning percentage of 93.4 during his career at IU, with 127 wins and only 9 losses. Ten IU wrestlers have had undefeated seasons.

Wrestler **Brian Dolph** was the Big Ten champion and an All–Big Ten selection in 1989 and 1990 at 150 pounds. He is shown here winning the 150-pound NCAA title in 1990. An All-American for three years, Dolph leads all Hoosier wrestlers with a career record of 127 victories and only 9 losses. He won the Gimbel Award in 1990.

(1914)

Men's Gymnastics

An Indiana University men's gymnastics team entered the Western Intercollegiate Meet in Chicago in the spring of 1914. The four members of the team were Archie Erehart (parallel bars), Dale Beeler (horizontal bars), and Chester Jones and Ralph Thompson (tumbling). The following year, IU did not participate in the meet; it lacked entrants in some of the events, and the competition was too far away, in Lincoln, Nebraska. IU did not take part in Big Ten gymnastics meets until 1942, when it placed fourth in a field of five. No meets were held from 1943 until 1947. The team had one of its best showings, placing fourth, in 1973, when the meet was held in Bloomington.

Dick Albershardt was the NCAA trampoline champion in 1956 and won the Big Ten title in this event in 1952, 1956, and 1957. Ron Walden was the Big Ten tumbling champion in 1959. Pat Kivland was an outstanding all-around performer in the late 1960s. Rings performer Benny Fernandez was an All-American and Big Ten champion during each of his four years (1971–1974) of competition, and his brother Landy won the Big Ten rings title in 1975. Pete Murao won back-to-back titles in the floor exercise in both the Big Ten and NCAA tournaments. Tim Connelly was an All–Big Ten performer on the pommel horse, and Tom Gould was All–Big Ten in the rings.

Jim Brown had been the coach for thirteen years when, at the end of the 1982 season, gymnastics was discontinued as a varsity sport. IU's highest placing at the Big Ten championships had been fourth, in 1972, 1973, and 1977. Nick Salano and Bernie Pratt were co-captains in the last year of varsity activity. The team had a roster of twenty-four men, nine of whom were lettermen, and was ranked 25th in the pre-season poll. Outstanding performers were Dan Stanley and Mike Hirsch.

In 1942, after a 28-year hiatus, the Indiana gymnastics team resumed competition in the Big Ten with a full complement of gymnasts. The team finished fourth in a field of five at the conference meet in Ann Arbor. From left to right: **Strodler**, **Ruflin**, **Green**, **Couchenour**, **Sarter**, **Coakley** (captain), and **Coach Schreiler**.

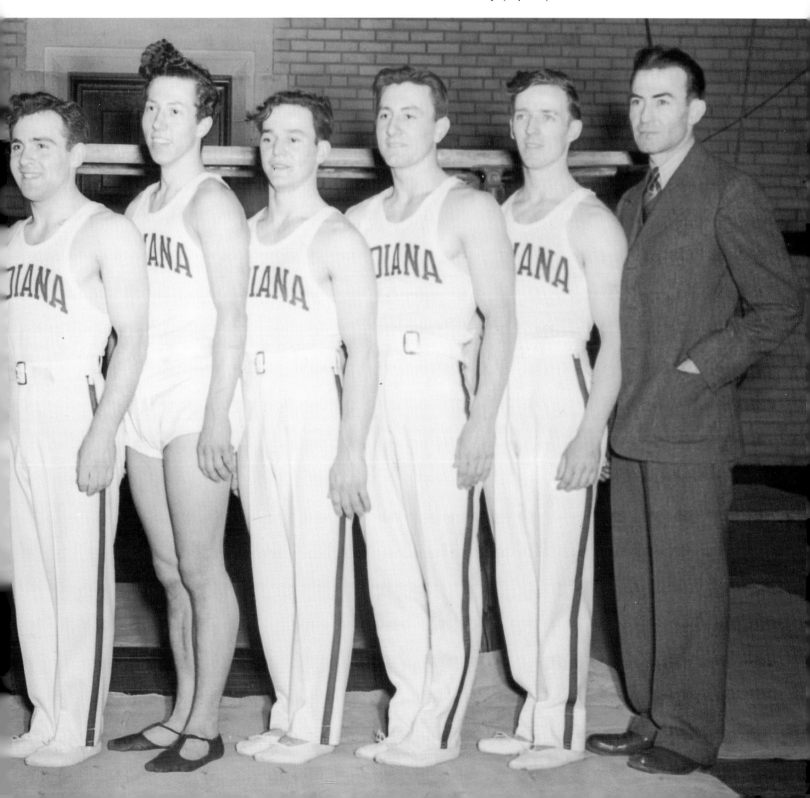

Dick Albershardt won the 1952 NCAA trampoline title, and was Big Ten champion in that event in 1952, 1956, and 1957. He later performed professionally under the name of Dick Albers.

Ron Walden was the Big Ten tumbling champion and the Big Ten Medal of Honor winner in 1959, and led the Hoosiers to many dual meet wins.

Benny Fernandez was an All-American performer on the rings, winning the Big Ten rings title in each of his seasons at IU (1971–1974). He won the Balfour Award in 1972, 1973, and 1974.

Pat Kivland, a member of the gymnastics team from 1967 to 1969, was one of Indiana's most outstanding performers on the rings and the parallel bars.

Varsity Sports at Indiana University

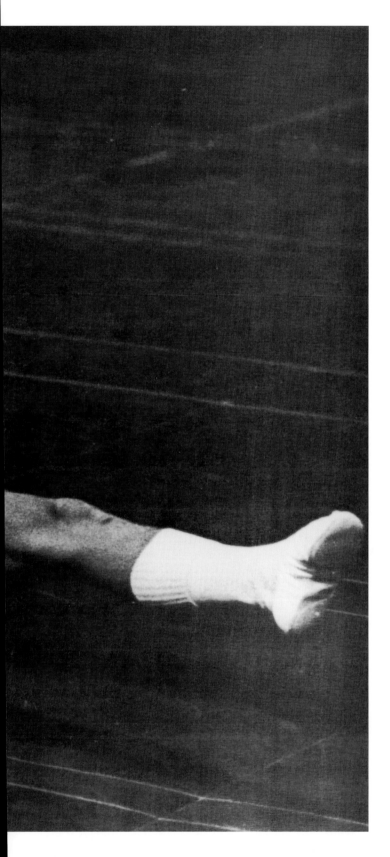

Pete Murao was the Big Ten and NCAA champion in the floor exercise event and an All-American gymnast in 1977 and 1978. In 1978 he won both the Balfour and Gimbel awards.

(1920)
Men's Swimming and Diving

IU's intramural swimming events were held at the old Assembly Hall or at the Student Building until 1917, when the new Men's Gymnasium opened. With a 30' x 90' swimming pool on its first floor, it remained the home of IU's swim team until 1962. In 1961, the Health, Physical Education and Recreation (HPER) Building was added to the north end of the Men's Gym and Fieldhouse. Within the structure was a large (76' x 45'), modern swimming pool with six swimming lanes and a diving area with one and three meter springboards and a one meter diving platform. It had seating for 1,600 spectators and was the state-of-the-art swimming and diving facility at that time. On March 3, 1962, the pool was dedicated to the memory of IU swimmer and coach Robert Royer. The Robert Royer Pool remained the home of the highly successful swimming Hoosiers until 1995.

An honorary swimming fraternity, Sigma Rho Tau, was founded at IU in 1919; in 1920 it had twenty-six members. It was the outgrowth of the old Dolphin Club. The 1920 swimming and diving team was the first to participate in an intercollegiate meet. Indiana's eight-man squad met teams from the Indianapolis and Cincinnati YMCAs, the Indianapolis Athletics Club, and Purdue University. They lost to all participants. The events at this

Robert Royer was a well-known national leader in intercollegiate swimming who served as Indiana's head coach for twenty-six years. A native Hoosier (he was born in a log cabin on a farm near Akron, Indiana), he entered IU in 1924 and earned his AB in English in 1928. While at IU, he took up swimming, and by his junior year he was one of the Big Ten's leading backstrokers. He moved back to Akron after graduation and taught there for two years before returning to Bloomington as head swimming coach in 1930. His duties at IU included teaching and administrative duties in the Office of the Dean of Men.

During his last few years at IU, Royer brought his swimmers to high national standing. His 1956 team tied for third in the Big Ten, and his 1957 squad was fourth in the NCAA. Three of his outstanding swimmers were Bill Woolsey, Dick "Sonny" Tanabe, and Frank McKinney, Jr. Each won a place on the 1956 U.S. Olympic swim team.

In 1947, the IU varsity swimming team adopted a mascot, "Driftwood I," a white decoy duck with a large crimson "I" painted on its back. The photo shows team captain **Dave McCooe** in the water with Driftwood I. In back are coach **Robert Royer**, **Charlie Snowden**, **Dick Brunoehler**, **George Cave**, and assistant coach **Bob Stumpner**; with their feet in the pool are **Rick Smith**, **Bob White**, **Ed Fulkman**, and **Tom Gastineau**.

pioneer event included 50, 100, and 200 yard freestyle races, a quarter-mile race, and breaststroke and backstroke races. Diving was included, most likely from a springboard.

Indiana's first swim coach was Guy L. Rathbun, who led the team in 1919 and 1920. He was succeeded by Robert Shafer and Lester Hill. William S. Merriam was the coach in 1923, when IU first entered a team in the Big Ten swimming and diving championship meet, held at the University of Chicago; the Hoosiers finished fifth in a field of eight. Oscar Tharp coached in 1925, and Merriam returned for another year in 1926. Paul Thompson was the coach from 1927 to 1930. The team was coachless in 1931, then was taken over by Robert Royer in 1932. He served until 1943 and was succeeded by Robert Stumpner, who coached for two years before Royer's return in 1946. Royer's teams had a dual meet record of 95 wins and 79 losses. His outstanding swimmers included Richard "Sonny" Tanabe, Bill Woolsey, and Frank McKinney, Jr.

Royer was succeeded by James "Doc" Counsilman in 1957. It took Counsilman, with his scientific methods, very few years to bring the IU swimmers to national prominence and to truly enrich the Indiana sports tradition. In 1959 and 1960, his tankmen finished second in the Big Ten and third in the NCAA meets. From 1961 through 1980, his swimmers won the Big Ten title every year, then placed second for two years before regaining the title for three additional years. His teams were runners-up in the NCAA in 1964, 1965, and 1966, and third in 1967 before winning the next six NCAA crowns. They then slipped to second place the two following years. During Counsilman's remarkable coaching career at Indiana from 1957 to 1990, his teams won 282 matches and lost only 33, for an amazing winning percentage of 89.5.

The list of Counsilman's Olympians reads like a Who's Who of swimming. Forty-six Counsilman-coached swimmers represented the United States at the Olympic Games from 1952 to 1988. Seventeen of those athletes won medals: twenty-nine gold, ten silver, and thirteen bronze. Counsilman was the coach of the U.S. Olympic team in 1964 and 1976.

The diving coach during the Counsilman years was Hobart "Hobie" Billingsley. His divers performed at the same high level as did Counsilman's swimmers. They won two gold and three bronze Olympic medals and eighteen individual Big Ten titles. Billingsley coached the U.S. Olympic divers in 1968. Jim Henry won three straight NCAA diving championships; other outstanding divers were Rick Gilbert and Ken Sitzberger.

One of the latest additions to Indiana's athletic facilities is now the home of the swimmers and divers. The $22,000,000 Student Recreational Sports Center, located on Law Lane, was dedicated in September 1995. The Counsilman Aquatic Center contains an eight-lane Olympic-sized pool with a depth of seven to eight feet, which results in the creation of less turbulence by the swimmers, and therefore permits better times. The Billingsley Diving Center houses one meter and three meter springboards in addition to one, three, five, seven, and ten meter diving platforms. The IU swimmers and divers also use the Natatorium, located on the Indianapolis campus, for meets.

Left: **Bill Woolsey** was IU's first great swimmer under Coach Royer. At the 1952 Olympics, he won a gold medal on the 800 meter freestyle relay team and participated in the 1,500 freestyle event. At the 1956 Olympics, he was a member of the silver medal–winning 800 meter freestyle relay team, and he also represented the U.S. in the 100 meter freestyle race. In 1956 and 1957, he won both the 220 and 440 yard freestyle events at the NCAA meet. Woolsey shared the Balfour Award with Sonny Tanabe in 1955 and 1956, then won it outright in 1957. He received the Gimbel Award in 1957.

Right: **Sonny Tanabe**, one of Coach Royer's recruits, was a member of the 1956 U.S. Olympic swimming team. At the NCAA meet in 1957, he set a new NCAA record (55.7 seconds) in the 100 meter butterfly in the qualifying round, but he placed second in the finals to Tim Jacko of Yale, who bettered Tanabe's mark with a time of 54.6 seconds. In the same meet, Tanabe finished third in the 200 meter individual medley, and swam the butterfly leg of IU's third-place medley relay team. In 1958, he set new varsity records in the 50 (:23.1) and 100 (:50.9) meter butterfly, and the 200 meter individual medley relay (2:08.0).

Frank McKinney, Jr., from Indianapolis, was one of IU's first premier swimmers. Young McKinney first met Doc Counsilman at the 1956 Olympics, where he won a bronze medal in the 100 meter backstroke event. He later helped recruit Counsilman to the coaching position at IU. At the 1960 Olympics, McKinney won a gold medal as a member of the 400 meter medley relay team and a silver medal in the 100 meter backstroke. He was elected to the International Swimming Hall of Fame in 1975.

Frank served on the IU Board of Trustees from 1973 to 1976. He was selected to receive the Clevenger Award in 1978. He was an active fundraiser for and supporter of the construction of the Counsilman swimming and the Billingsley diving complex at the Student Recreational Sports Center on the campus.

McKinney was killed in a plane crash in 1992 while serving as the chairman and CEO of Bank One in Indianapolis. In June of 1997, the Frank E. McKinney, Jr. Fountain of the Bess Meshulan Simon Center (formerly University High School and the School of Education Building) was dedicated in his honor. It stands on the South Mezzanine of the Musical Arts Center on Jordan Avenue.

Jim "Doc" Counsilman, a native of Birmingham, Alabama, earned his BS in physical education at Ohio State, where he won a Big Ten championship in the breaststroke. He later earned an MS in exercise physiology at Illinois and a PhD at Iowa. He taught and coached at Cortland State Teachers College in Cortland, New York, before coming to IU in 1957 to be the head swimming coach.

Counsilman's teams have brought home twenty-three Big Ten titles, and they won six consecutive NCAA crowns. Many of his swimmers have earned national and international acclaim, including George Breen, Gary Hall, Charlie Hickox, Chet Jastremski, John Kinsella, Don McKenzie, Frank McKinney, Jr., Jim Montgomery, John Murphy, Fred Schmidt, Larry Schulhof, Alan Somers, Mark Spitz, Ted Stickles, and Mike Troy. Doc is the author of many scientific articles and several books and manuals on training methods and biomechanical principles and theories as they relate to swimming; his highly regarded book *The Science of Swimming* has been translated into more than twenty languages.

Counsilman attracted the world's attention when, at the age of fifty-eight, he successfully swam the English Channel.

Olympian **Rick Gilbert** was one of Hobie Billingsley's early diving stars. As a freshman in 1962, he won the National AAU three meter platform event. Gilbert won the Big Ten one meter title in 1963, and both the one and three meter titles in 1964 and 1965. He won the three meter AAU title in 1961, 1962, and 1963, and the one meter title in 1963. In 1964, he won the NCAA one meter dive. In 1965, Gilbert participated in the World University Games in Budapest, winning both the three and ten meter titles. He added the three and ten meter AAU outdoor titles to his record in 1966. Gilbert has been the diving coach at Cornell University since 1968. In 1986 he was named Men's Diving Coach of the Year.

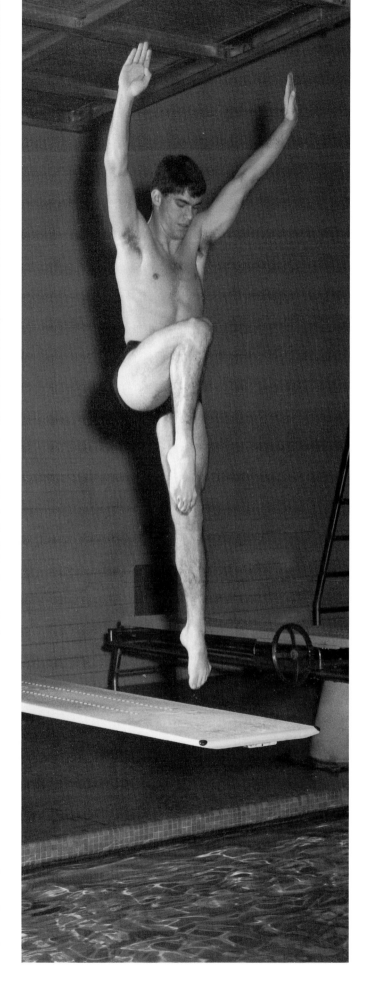

Ken Sitzberger was another of Hobie Billingsley's outstanding divers. At the 1964 Olympics, he won the gold medal in the springboard competition. Sitzberger won the NCAA one and three meter events in 1965, 1966, and 1967, and was the U.S. indoor champion in those events in 1964 and 1965. He won the Big Ten Medal of Honor in 1967.

Hobie Billingsley was Indiana's first diving coach. Billingsley graduated from Ohio State in 1951, where he was elected to the All-American diving team on four occasions for his performances on both the low and high boards. In 1953 he earned an MS from the University of Washington. He spent the next several years barnstorming throughout the United States with his diving acrobatics and trick routines, before assuming his post at IU on May 6, 1959.

Billingsley coached sixteen of his divers to NCAA titles, including such outstanding athletes as Rick Gilbert, Jim Henry, Ken Sitzberger, Kim Young, Rich Early, Leslie Bush, Cynthia Potter, Amy McGrath, Kristen Kane, Rob Bollinger, Lona Foss, and Mark Lenzi. He was the Diving Coach of the Year in 1964, 1965, and 1966, and Olympic diving coach in 1968, 1976, and 1980. Billingsley and Doc Counsilman were among the first to apply basic biomechanical principles and the laws of physics to the technics of diving.

At the 1961 Big Ten swimming championships, the Indiana swimmers won their first of 23 conference titles under Coach Counsilman. Alan Somers set a Big Ten record in the 1,500 meter freestyle and NCAA and Big Ten records in the 440 meter freestyle. John Roethe and Mike Troy set Big Ten records in the 200 meter individual medley and the 200 meter butterfly, respectively. Frank McKinney set U.S., NCAA, and Big Ten records in the 200 meter backstroke, and a Big Ten record in the 100 meter backstroke. Peter Sintz won the 220 freestyle. Chet Jastremski placed second in the 100 and 200 meter breaststroke and the 200 meter individual medley events. Dick Beaver and Terry Laberdie were runners-up in the 200 meter backstroke and 100 meter butterfly, respectively. Third place winners were John Roethke (100 meter backstroke), Mike Troy (100 meter butterfly and 440 freestyle), and Jim Fitzgibbon (50 meter freestyle). Ken Nakasone, Frank McKinney, Terry Laberdie, and Tom Verth teamed to finish second in the 400 meter medley relay, and the 400 meter freestyle team of Bill Cass, Jim Fitzgibbon, Terry Laberdie, and Paul Sintz took third place.

First row, left to right: **David Smith**, **Richard Kitchell**, **Keith Craddock**, **William Barton**, and **John Roethke**; second row: **Larry Hoo**, **Peter Sintz**, **Richard Beaver**, **Frank McKinney**, **Terry Laberdie**, **Chet Jastremski**, and **James Fitzgibbon**; third row: diving coach **Hobie Billingsley**, **Jerry Holtrey**, **Henry Miki**, **Roy Lovstedt**, **John Walker**, **Ken Nakasone**, **William Marks**, and coach **Jim Counsilman**; top row: manager **Jack Boehm**, **Herbert Hebb**, **William Cass**, **John Odusch**, **Mike Troy**, **Tom Verth**, **Alan Somers**, and manager **Ron Davitt**.

Mike Troy competed at the 1960 Olympics, where he won gold in the 200 meter butterfly and as a member of the U.S. 800 meter freestyle relay team. He helped win the 400 meter medley relay at the 1959 Pan American Games. Troy won the NCAA 100 and 200 meter butterfly crown in 1960, and teamed with Frank McKinney, Gerry Miki, and Peter Sintz to capture the 400 meter medley relay event. He won five individual National AAU butterfly events and two individual Big Ten titles in the butterfly. He received the Balfour Award in 1962.

Charlie Hickox began his swimming career at IU in 1967. He was the NCAA champion in the 100 and 200 meter backstroke event two years in a row. He won four medals at the 1968 Olympics: gold in the 200 and 400 meter races and in the 400 meter medley relay, and silver in the 100 meter backstroke. Hickox received the Balfour Award in 1968 and 1969.

Varsity Sports at Indiana University

At the 1968 NCAA Indoor Swimming and Diving Championships in Greenville, North Carolina, Indiana won its first of six straight titles by beating the second-place Santa Clara Swim Club 334 to 269. Jim Henry won the one meter diving competition, with Win Young second and alum Dick Gilbert third. Young won the three meter event (Gilbert was second), and Henry placed fourth in the ten meter competition. Leslie Bush won the platform and three meter events and finished fifth in the one meter board dive.

Charlie Hickox won the 100 and 200 meter backstroke and the 200 meter individual medley (Bill Utley placed 3rd), and Bill Burrell won the 200 meter freestyle. Utley placed second in the 400 meter individual medley, and three relay teams placed in the top three.

Front row, left to right: manager **Terry Weisman, Win Young, Jim Henry, Dave Perkowski,** co-captains **Bill Utley** and **Luis Nini de Rivera, Nick Carlton, Jon Hahnfeldt,** and manager **Jeff Bankston;** middle row: coach **Jim Counsilman, Dave Bayles, Fred Southward, Charlie Hickox, Bryan Bateman, Dave Usrey, Don McKenzie, Tito Perez,** and coach **Hobie Billingsley;** back row: manager **Mark Wallace, Bobby Windle, Bill Burrell, Ron Jacks, Steve Ware, Steve Borowski,** manager **Corby Sanders,** and assistant coach **Jack Pettinger.**

Mark Spitz accomplished an amazing feat in winning seven events at the 1972 Olympics. He took home the gold in the 100 and 200 meter freestyle, the 100 and 200 meter butterfly, the 400 meter medley relay, the 400 meter freestyle relay, and the 800 meter freestyle relay. He also was the NCAA champion in his specialties in 1969, 1970, 1971, and 1972. In 1971, Spitz set seven world and two U.S. swimming records, winning four national and two collegiate championship events. He was an All–Big Ten and All-American swimmer throughout his career. Spitz was the Sullivan Award winner in 1971.

Gary Hall set nine individual world records in the butterfly, backstroke, and individual medley events. He was the World Swimmer of the Year in 1969 and 1970. Hall swam in three Olympics: 1968, 1972, and 1976. He won a silver medal in the 400 meter race in 1968, a silver in the 200 meter butterfly in 1972, and a bronze in the 100 meter butterfly in 1976. He was captain of the U.S. Olympic swim team in 1972 and 1976. He also won seven individual NCAA swimming championships.

After graduating from medical school at the University of Cincinnati, Hall finished his residency in ophthalmology at the IU Medical Center in 1982. Dr. Hall is the author of four books on eyesight. He heads the Hall Eye Surgery Institute in Arizona, and is the spokesman for the National Society to Prevent Blindness.

Hall was awarded the Big Ten Medal of Honor in 1973. In 1997, he received an NCAA Silver Anniversary Award, which acknowledges athletes who have distinguished themselves in the twenty-five years since finishing their collegiate careers.

Mike Stamm was an outstanding performer at the 1972 Olympics. He was on the winning 400 meter medley relay team with Mark Spitz, and won silver medals in the 100 and 200 meter backstroke events. In 1973, he won the NCAA crown in the 100 and 200 meter backstroke.

John Kinsella won a gold medal at the 1972 Olympics as a member of the 800 meter freestyle relay team. He won six individual NCAA championships, five National AAU titles, and numerous Big Ten championships in 1971, 1972, and 1973 in his specialty, the distance swims between 500 and 1,650 meters. In 1973 he teamed with Gary Hall, Fred Tyler, and Gary Conelly to win the NCAA 800 meter freestyle relay, and in 1974 with Tyler, Jim Montgomery, and Tom Hickox to win the 400 meter freestyle relay.

Kinsella was the AAU's Sullivan Award winner as the nation's outstanding amateur athlete in 1970.

Olympic gold medalist **Mark Lenzi** earned his BS from IU in 1990. Lenzi won the NCAA one meter board competition in 1989 and 1990; he was the U.S. outdoor champion in the one meter event in 1991, the U.S. indoor three meter champion in 1991, and the one and three meter champion in 1992. He was the World Cup Champion Diver in 1989 and 1991. He also won four Big Ten championships. He won the gold medal in the one meter dive at the Pan American Games in 1991, then won the gold medal in the three meter diving competition at the 1992 Olympics at Barcelona. Lenzi came out of retirement in 1995. Despite suffering several injuries in training, under the tutelage of Hobie Billingsley he captured the bronze medal at the 1996 Olympics in Atlanta.
Photo copyright © by Dave Repp.

Men's Swimming and Diving   117

Men's Golf

In 1899, IU created a six-hole golf course south of East 10th Street between Jordan and Woodlawn Avenues. It occupied what is now the Arboretum, the site of the first Memorial Stadium, and the old Parade Ground used by the ROTC. This very imperfectly developed acreage was named the Dunn Meadow Golf Club. It had about fifty members; faculty members were charged $5.00 and students $1.50 per season for the privilege of playing there. The first college golf course in the state, it attracted much interest on the campus and in the city of Bloomington. It is said to have influenced the Bloomington city fathers to construct the municipal course at the Cascades.

The IU men's golf team was formed in 1924. During that season, the team played all of its matches on the road, because it had no home course. It lost to Illinois, Michigan, Notre Dame, and Purdue. Some of the team members participated in the Big Ten championship match held in Chicago, but because the team was not complete, their scores were not recorded. Golf was not well supported financially during the early years. The Blue Key and Sphinx Clubs occasionally contributed funds for "I" sweaters and traveling expenses. Players supplied their own equipment and golf balls.

For some years, all of the team's home matches were played at the Bloomington Country Club. On June 24, 1957, the new eighteen-hole Indiana University Golf Course opened for play. Carved out of a 250-acre tract of wooded watershed land on the far northeast side of the campus, it is a course of great beauty that tests the skills of the most talented golfers. The Indiana University Golf Complex, in addition to the eighteen-hole, 6,700-yard championship course, has a nine-hole par three course. A lighted driving range, a clubhouse, locker space, and an automatic sprinkling system have been added. The clubhouse was named for Harold Wegmiller, who left money for that purpose. It was thirty-three years after men's intercollegiate golf was added to the IU sports program before the IU men had their own course on which to practice and compete.

Five years after intercollegiate golf competition started at IU, the team won the State Intercollegiate Meet at DePauw in 1929. The victorious team had no official coach, for in the early years of golf, one of the student athletes acted as player-manager-coach: Harper Miller, Phil Talbot, Francis Cox, Phil Greenwood, and Charles Harrell served in that capacity The first (1934) non-playing coach was Hugh E. Willis, a professor of law. In 1942, James Soutar, golf professional at the Bloomington Country Club (and one of the designers of the present course), became the golf coach; he was followed by Owen L. Cochran.

Robert B. Fitch served as golf coach from 1957 to 1981, and under his direction the team placed first in the Big Ten in 1962, 1968, 1970, 1973, 1974, and 1975. Byron Comstock was Indiana's first Big Ten medalist, in 1964; Don Pagett, Jr., won the title in 1969. Wayne McDonald was an All-American in 1969 and 1970, and Kelly Roberts was an All-American selection in 1974. Bob Ackerman and Gary Biddinger were co-medalists at the

The 1931 Indiana University golf team consisted of four members. From left to right: **Phil Talbot** of Bloomington, **Francis "Fritz" Cox** of Evansville, **Phil Greenwood** of Washington, Indiana, and **Charlie Harrell** of Bloomington. The team finished third in the state meet, which was held in Terre Haute. Greenwood served as captain and coach for the 1931 team; Talbot coached the 1932 golfers; and Harrell was coach for the 1933 team. Greenwood and Harrell both became attorneys. Harrell served as IU's registrar and as secretary of the Board of Trustees.

In 1962, Indiana won its first men's Big Ten golf title in Champaign, topping second-place Purdue by a score of 1,509 to 1,514. Phil White placed sixth, to lead the Hoosier golfers with a score of 298. Tom Thomas was 8th with 300, and Byron Comstock followed at 10th with 301. Also placing were Charlie Griffith (22nd), Jerry McRae (30th), and Forest Jones (42nd). Coach Bob Fitch's team had a record of 13 wins, 3 losses, and 1 tie in dual meets.

Kneeling, left to right: **Jerry McRae**, **Gordon Lane**, **Berry Cooper**, **Charles Griffith**, and **Byron Comstock**; standing: coach **Bob Fitch**, **Fred Henoch**, **Forest Jones**, **Phil White**, and **Tom Thomas**.

Fitch, a former football All-American and world record holder in the discus, first came to IU in 1952 as end coach for the football team. In 1958 he took over as golf coach, inheriting a team that had consistently ranked near the bottom of the Big Ten. That year IU moved up from tenth to second in the conference, with Ron Boyer, Jon Sommer, and Phil Kreite as the leading scorers. Fitch's teams won Big Ten titles in 1962, 1968, 1970, 1974, and 1975, and made twelve NCAA appearances. He helped develop such players as Byron Comstock, Don Pagett, Jr., Wayne McDonald, Kelley Roberts, Bob Ackerman, Gary Biddinger, Rob Jackson, Ted Koressel, and Mike Ingram.

Big Ten Meet in 1975, followed by Mike Ingram in 1984 and Shaun Micheel in 1991. Sam Carmichael, the present coach, succeeded Hicks; his 1991 team placed first in the Big Ten, and he was named Big Ten Coach of the Year. That same year, the IU team of Shaun Micheel, Bill Miller, Kyle Wienek, Jody Roudebush, and Joe Tomaselle posted the record low score in the Big Ten championship meet; Micheel's 276 for 72 holes was the third-lowest individual score in Big Ten history. Since 1968, thirty Hoosier golfers have been selected to the All–Big Ten team. Micheel was the Big Ten Player of the Year in 1991, and Randy Leen won the same honor in 1996 and 1997.

The 1968 golf team captured the Big Ten title, besting Michigan State in the four-round tourney by a score of 1,511 to 1,523. IU had a season dual meet record of 24 wins, 3 losses, and 1 tie. Steve Cisco was the tournament runner-up, finishing two strokes behind medalist Bill Brasck of Minnesota with a score of 295; Jim Cheney, Ron Essenpreis, Dan May, and Bill Stinnet added points to the winning total for IU.

Left to right: **Jim Cheney**, **Wayne McDonald**, **Dan May**, **Walt Osterberg**, **Ron Essenpreis**, **Steve Cisco**, **Rick Lee**, **Bill Stinnett**, and coach **Bob Fitch**.

In 1969, **Don Pagett, Jr.,** won the Big Ten tourney, with a four-round total of 290, and was named to the All–Big Ten team. His son Don Pagett III finished in a tie for 5th in the 1996 Big Ten tourney.

(1952)

Men's Rifle

According to the 1996 *Directory of Indiana University I-Men*, letters in rifle were awarded at IU for only five seasons—1952/53 through 1956/57. The *Arbutus* covered the activities of the rifle team beginning in 1948, but discontinued it after 1969. The 1951/52 team was the undefeated champion of the Big Ten. The team captain the following year was Verle Wright, Jr. In 1968, Indiana University's rifle team captured the Big Ten crown again, by scoring 2,690 points out of a possible 3,000.

The 1953 rifle team won the Big Ten competition in marksmanship, led by Verle Wright. Kneeling, left to right: **Stan Collins, Charles Massa, Verle Wright, Alonzo Boyd**, and **James Dartnell**; standing: **Captain Donotto, Roger Burton, Jackie Jones, Marvin Huntsinger, Robert Thomas, William McEwin, Terry Edgeworth**, and **Sgt. R. C. Bates**.

Men's Rifle

Verle Wright, Jr., was the captain of the 1953 rifle team. He led the Big Ten in marksmanship and was an All-American rifleman. He was a member of the 1952 U.S. Olympic team, winning a gold medal in the small bore competition as he set a world record. As Lieutenant Wright, he again won a gold medal in the small bore competition at the 1956 Olympic Games. He is shown here with teammate **Alonzo Boyd**.

The 1967/68 Big Ten champion IU rifle team is pictured here showing President Elvis Stahr the Russel Mill Trophy. From left to right: **Major Edward D. Lyerley** (officer in charge), **Don Adams**, **Tom Wilson**, **President Stahr**, **Phil Huffman**, **Bruce Woodard**, **Cliff Culloden**, **John Mitchell**, and **Staff Sergeant Jim North**, the team's coach.

(1962)

Women's Basketball

In the early years, the rules of women's basketball demanded that a "three line game" be played. The playing court was divided into three sections, with the play of the centers restricted to the middle portion of the court, forwards to the offensive portion, and guards to the defensive end. The rules for women's basketball are now the same as those for men.

According to the *Arbutus*, interclass basketball was the first form of athletics in which IU women participated. In 1897, coed class basketball teams held exhibition games in Wylie Hall, where the ceiling of the court was very low. The contests were then moved to Mitchell Hall, where the presence of six pillars in the court tended to impede play. The first truly intercollegiate women's basketball game was played in 1905. The next varsity team was not formed until 1962.

Under coach Bea Gorton (1971–1979), the women of IU compiled a record of 79 wins and only 29 losses, for a winning percentage of 73.1. Joy Malchodi's teams had a 52.6 winning percentage over the next four years. Maryalyce Jeremiah coached the next five years, compiling a record of 90 and 63; her 1983 team tied for the Big Ten championship and advanced to the NCAA Regional Finals. Jeremiah was succeeded by Jorja Hoehn, whose teams posted a 47 percent winning rate.

The present coach, Jim Izard, has re-established the winning tradition of the Cream and Crimson women hoopsters. The 1991 team placed second in the 1991 National Invitational Tournament, losing to Santa Clara by a score of 71 to 68 in the finals, and the 1994 and 1995 teams were invited to play in the NCAA tournament. Izard's 1997 team was defeated in the semi-finals of the Big Ten tournament by the eventual champion, Iowa. His teams have a record of 128 and 98.

Standout players for the women Hoosiers have included Tara VanDerVeer, Debbie Oing, Denise Jackson, Karna Abram, Cindy Bumgarner, Lisa Furlin, Rachelle Bostic, Zandrea Jefferies, Shirley Bryant, Tisha Hill, Sue Hodges, Quacy Barnes, Kristi Green, and Sarah Warner.

The 1973 women's basketball team, coached by Bea Gorton, had a record of 17 wins and only 3 defeats. They won the state and regional AIAW titles and advanced to the final four in the nationals, but lost in the semifinals to Queens College. The team had no athletic scholarships; women basketball players did not receive athletic scholarships until 1976/77.

Front row, left to right: **Jane Christopherson**, **Linda Whitt, Jo Price**, and **Debbie Oing**; back row: **Carol Kegley**, **Lou Stevenson**, **Jorja Hoehn**, **Terri Winchester, Tara VanDerVeer,** and **Pat Wakefield**.

While coaching at Ohio State, Tara VanDerVeer was the Big Ten Coach of the Year in 1984 and 1985. At Stanford she was the PAC Ten Coach of the Year in 1989, 1990, and 1995, and the National Coach of the Year in 1988, 1989, and 1995. Jorja Hoehn coached the Lady Hoosiers from 1985 through 1988. Sophomore Debbie Oing was on the All-American women's basketball team in 1975, and has been elected, along with VanDerVeer, to the Hoosier Hall of Fame.

The 1983 women's basketball team shared the Big Ten title with Ohio State. Denise Jackson, Rachelle Bostic, and Linda Cunningham led IU to the championship with help from Debbie McClure and Julie Kronenberger. Melissa Leckie and Melinda Sparkman added good balance. Senior co-captain Kim Land was lost to the team because of a broken foot. The Lady Hoosiers had a season record of 19 and 11, but their Big Ten record was 15 and 3. They won the conference title by beating OSU 62 to 56 in the final game of the season. They advanced to the NCAA tourney and won IU's first-ever first-round game in NCAA competition by beating Kentucky 87 to 76, but they lost in the Mideast Regional Tourney to Georgia.

Front row, left to right: **Randy Mascorella, Linda Cunningham, Kim Land, Denise Jackson, Amy Matheny, Jennifer Wilfong**, and assistant coach **June Kearney**; middle row: trainer **Sue Hannam, Kemya Willis, Sue Watts, Melissa Leckie, Pam Mach, Paula McDaley, Debbie McClure**, and trainer **Jeanna Polonchek**; back row: coach **Maryalyce Jeremiah**, manager **Pat Flynn, Melinda Sparkman, Rachelle Bostic, Julie Kronenberger, Kelly Bynum**, and manager **Laura Spless**.

Denise Jackson leads all Indiana University women's basketball scorers with a total of 1,917 points during her four-year career (1981–1984). She led the team with 366 rebounds in 1983 and had a team high of 1,263, 10.3 per game, during her career. She hit a record 15 free throws in a game against Wisconsin in 1982, led the team with 160 in 1983, and made the most free throws, 642, during her career. She was an All–Big Ten Player in 1981, 1983, and 1984.

Jackson, number 12, is shown here rebounding against Kentucky, with **Debbie McClure** on the left, and **Linda Cunningham** blocking out on the right. Cunningham was also a great scorer, with 1,169 points in 114 games.

Rachelle Bostic, who played both forward and center for IU from 1981 to 1984, leads all Lady Hoosier basketball players with her total of 839 field goals scored during her career. Her average of 15.99 points per game and her total of 1,827 points put her fourth among the lady hoopsters. The 6' Bostic led the team in scoring during the 1984 season, with game totals of 38 points against South Carolina and 34 points against Michigan. She captained the Big Ten co-championship team in 1983.

Above: **Karna Abram**, a 6'2" forward, played basketball at IU from 1984 to 1987. She stands second in career scoring, with 1,910 points. Her 642 points (22.9 per game) in 1985 and 626 points (23.2 per game) in 1987 lead all Hoosiers. Abram's top scoring efforts were 39 points against Illinois in 1985, and 40 against Michigan State and 39 against Michigan in 1987. She led the team in scoring in 1985, 1986, and 1987, shooting .510 from the field the last year. She won All–Big Ten honors in 1985, 1986, and 1987, and was the Varsity Club Scholar Athlete of the Year in 1986.

Opposite: **Cindy Bumgarner** played basketball for IU from 1985 to 1988. She leads all IU women's basketball players in scoring average, with 17.3 points per game, and ranks third in career points, with 1,836. On three occasions she scored 30 or more points in a game. Bumgarner was an effective rebounder and shot-blocker who also led the team each year in free throw percentage; her 86.0 percentage in 1988 is IU's highest. She was selected to the All–Big Ten first team in 1986.

Zandrea "Zan" Jefferies was an outstanding member of the basketball team from 1988 to 1991. She scored a total of 1,173 points, for an average of 10.3 per game. She was a great rebounder (769 in her career) and was a leader in steals (172) and assists. In 1990 she had 62 steals and 243 rebounds. Jefferies was named to the All–Big Ten second team in 1990 and 1991.

(1962)

Women's Field Hockey

Intramural women's field hockey was a popular sport on the Bloomington campus as early as 1911. The games were played on Dunn Meadow. When women's field hockey became a varsity sport in 1962, games were played on the IU football practice field. Kay Burrus was the coach then, and her teams had a winning record for thirteen consecutive years. In 1976, only two team members, Chris Archer and Cynthia Bustard, were tendered athletes for the eleven starting positions on the team. A recruit from the East with extensive high school playing experience, Nancy Chubb, added depth and skill to the team in 1977. Chubb was the first IU competitor to be selected to the U.S. field hockey squad. Pat Fabozzi

In the twelfth year of women's field hockey at IU, the 1973/74 team compiled a record of 6 wins, 6 losses, and 2 ties. Front row, left to right: **Shela Northcutt, Lynda Rourke, Elaine Felfius, Julie Frank, Cindy Clements, Diana Okon, Kathy Krone, Mary-beth Hoey, Kathy LaPlante**, and coach **Kay Burrus**; back row: **Cathy Meyer, Jodee Richarson, Debbie Kuhlmeier, Mary Maher, Chris Archer, Evelyn Butler, Rosie Oberting, Tammy Williams, Diane Singer, Martha Wolf**, and **Shery Servin**.

Center halfback **Mary Maher**, on the right, surveys the field while **Elaine Felfius**, on the left, evades the action between two DePauw defenders. IU won the game, 3 to 0.

replaced Burrus as the coach in 1977; she was followed by Patty Foster, who led the team during the last year (1982) of the varsity squad's existence. The team finished third in the unofficial Big Ten standings in 1979, led by co-captains Margie Morgan and Cindy Jaworski ("the Polish Cannon"), goalie Angie Paul, and top scorer Sue Garnier.

In 1981, the team found a home playing field in the infield of the Billy Hayes Track; they finished second in the Indiana AIAW, and hosted the Midwest AIAW Tourney.

The university discontinued its support of field hockey in the spring of 1982. At that time, the squad had twelve tendered athletes. Support for those remaining at IU continued through the 1984/85 academic year. In 2000, women's field hockey will return as a varsity sport at IU.

Indiana University finished second in the Big Ten in 1978, and fourth in the 1981 Big Ten Tournament. The Hoosiers won the Indiana AIAW crown in both 1981 and 1982, and placed third in the Regional AIAW Meet in

Action in a 1977/78 field hockey game shows **Ann Englund** (*left*), **Barb Chesstal** (*right*), and **Cindy Jaworski**, "the Polish Cannon," taking a shot. Sue Garnier, an outstanding defensive player, and Pam Mitchell, a generator of offense, led the team to a 17 and 3 season. Indiana finished first in the Big Ten, second in the Indiana AIAW, and third in the Midwest AIAW under Coach Pat Fabozzi.

1982. Shari Schaftlein was IU's leading scorer in 1982, with 20 goals. The overall record of Indiana's short-lived varsity field hockey team was 48 wins, 48 losses, and 8 ties.

Currently, only six teams in the Big Ten compete in field hockey: Iowa, Michigan, Michigan State, Northwestern, Ohio State, and Penn State.

Nancy Chubb came to Indiana from Massachusetts in 1974. With five years of field hockey experience, she added skill, precision, and depth to Coach Kay Burrus's team. In 1974, she became the first IU field hockey player to be selected to the U.S. field hockey team. She scored four goals in a shutout game for IU in 1975, and was selected to the All-Midwest Women's Field Hockey Team.

This photograph was taken during the last season (1981) of intercollegiate competition for IU's women's varsity field hockey team. The Hoosiers are on the attack, with **Karen Norris** (*left*) closing in on the ball. Other IU players, in the white blouses, include **Laura Demers, Lexie deVries, Jackie Hagenbach**, and **Connie Walton**. There were twelve tendered student/athletes on the squad of twenty-two women.

Women's Volleyball

A women's volleyball team was established at IU in 1966. It became very active in 1970, then won the state championship in 1971. The Athletic Department began to help finance the program in 1972. In 1973, under coach Louetta Bloecher, the team posted a 13 and 6 record and placed second in the state tournament, losing only to champion Ball State. Margaret Schaufelberger coached the Hoosiers to a state championship in 1974. Ann Lawver became the coach in 1975, and under her leadership the team won the AIAW state championship tourney, entered the Midwest AIAW Regional Tournament, and placed third in the unofficial Big Ten championship held at Minneapolis. Lawver's teams had a record of 158 victories, 148 losses, and 9 ties during her eight seasons at IU. Doug West became the volleyball coach in 1983. He led the team for four years, then was succeeded by Tom Shoji. West's teams won 48 percent of their games; Shoji's six-year stint as coach resulted in a 47.5 percent winning record. In 1993, Katie Weismiller, who had coached at St. Louis University, took the helm.

In 1981, the Big Ten recommended that women's athletics be incorporated into its varsity sports activities. The 1981 Big Ten volleyball championship tourney was held at the University of Illinois on October 23–24, and was won by Michigan. In 1985, the conference champion was determined by a ten-week round-robin schedule. The winner of the conference is awarded an automatic berth in the NCAA Championship playoffs, and Indiana was one

Joy Jordan played volleyball from 1987 to 1990. She was the Varsity Club Scholar Athlete in 1989 and 1990, an Academic All–Big Ten member in 1988, 1989, and 1990, and an Academic All-American in 1990, winning the Big Ten Medal of Honor in 1991. Jordan had 899 digs in her career.

The 1986 volleyball team, coached by Doug West, had a record of 18 and 13, finishing fifth in the Big Ten with a record of 9 and 9. Front row, left to right: **Karen Dunham, Kim Hairston, Patti Zumerchik, Angie Hunter, Patty Dunham**, and **Andra Walker**; back row: **Jill Beggs, Mary Jo Waddell, Karen Knoll, Liz Armbrustmacher, Julie Goedde**, and **Lisa John**.

Liz Armbrustmacher, Karen Dunham, and Julie Goedde received Big Ten honorable mention in 1987. Armbrustmacher repeated the honor in 1988, and Goedde earned it again in 1989. Dunham, Goedde, Lisa John, Karen Knoll, and Patti Zumerchik all made Academic All–Big Ten during their careers.

of the five Big Ten teams to be invited to the tournament that year.

The 1995 Hoosiers tied for fourth in the Big Ten standings, with a 12 and 8 record. Junior Julie Flatley, one of IU's outside hitters, was named to the All–Big Ten team, and sophomore Jennifer Magelssen received honorable mention.

The team's home matches were played alternately at Assembly Hall and the old University High School gym until 1996, when they were moved to the Intercollegiate Athletic Gym (IAG), located adjacent to the intersection of 10th Street and the State Road 45/46 bypass. The renovated gym seats 2,500 and has new locker rooms and training rooms. Its state-of-the-art playing surface, "Sports Court," consists of thousands of interlocking plastic squares that rest on a layer of felt.

The 1997 season began with Indiana winning a record 15 straight games. The team went on to finish the season with a record of 18 and 15, however, placing eighth in the Big Ten.

Among the recent players who have contributed heavily to the volleyball program are Liz Armbrustmacher,

Lynn Crawley, Karen Dunham, Anne Eastman, Julie Goedde, Joy Jordan, and Michelle McElroy.

In the fall of 1975 the Monon Spike Match was created, and it has become as much a symbol to Hoosier and Boilermaker women volleyballers as the Old Oaken Bucket is to the IU and Purdue football teams. Purdue leads Indiana in the Monon Spike series, sixteen victories to eight, but IU has won four of the last six games.

Julie Goedde played volleyball for IU from 1986 to 1989. She was an All–Big Ten and All-Mideast Region selection in 1989, earning the Big Ten Medal of Honor. Goedde leads all IU players in block-assists (393), block-solos (128), and total blocks. She is second on the all-time list for kills (1,280) and digs (1,013), and had 110 service aces.

Karen Dunham had 154 service aces during her four years of play at IU. She ranked high in assists, digs, and blocks. Dunham was the Big Ten Freshman of the Year in 1984 and was a four-time All–Big Ten player (first team in 1985 and second team in 1984, 1986, and 1987). She was a two-time Varsity Club Scholar Athlete, in 1986 and 1987. An Academic All–Big Ten performer, she was awarded the Big Ten Medal of Honor in 1988.

Liz Armbrustmacher was a star with the IU volleyball team from 1985 to 1988. She leads all IU players in kills, with 1,381 during her career. Armbrustmacher was also an excellent server, with a total of 134 aces, and an outstanding blocker, second only to Julie Goedde with a total of 417 blocks. She was an outstanding team leader. She was the Big Ten Player of the Week on two occasions.

Anne Eastman was an All–Big Ten volleyball player in 1993 and 1994, and was on the All-Mideast second team in 1994. She was also an Academic All–Big Ten player, earning the Varsity Club Scholar Athlete Award in 1994, as well as the Big Ten Medal of Honor. She led the team in total blocks in 1993 and 1994, and in kills (539) and digs (319) in 1994.

Women's Golf

IU women first participated in intercollegiate golf matches in 1968, as part of the extramural program sponsored by the Department of Physical Education for Women. Initially the competition was restricted to matches within the state of Indiana. The budget for the women's golf team for the 1969/70 season was $40.00; it was increased to $47.60 the following year. The Department of Physical Education for Women was responsible for the funding of all women's intercollegiate athletic programs until the end of the 1974 academic year, after which the Department of Intercollegiate Athletics assumed the funding for all women's sports at IU. In 1976/77, there were four tendered women athletes in golf: Sally Hendron, Victoria Lakoff, Susan Schilling, and Donna Betner. Margaret Cummins coached the team through 1978.

In 1977, the women golfers finished third in an informal Big Ten tournament. They finished fourth in 1978, then second in 1979 at the championship meet held at Michigan State.

Sam Carmichael became the coach of the team in 1981. The IU women have since won six Big Ten team titles and finished second on six occasions. IU women have won the individual Big Ten title six times. Both the coach and the players have been showered with honors. Erika Wicoff is the most recent outstanding IU women's golfer. Others include Sarah DeKraay, Michele Redman, Shannon Hardesty, Debbie Lee, Tracy Chapman, and Amy McDonald.

The IU women golfers won their first Big Ten title in May 1986. The team had won the Illinois State Invitational, the Lady Northern Invitational, the Lady Buckeye Invitational, and the Iowa Invitational. In the Big Ten meet held in Ann Arbor, IU beat out second-place Minnesota in the four-round event by a score of 1,250 to 1,308. Sarah DeKraay led the Hoosier lady golfers, winning the meet with a four-round score of 313. She was followed by Tracy Chapman, second (314); Michele Redman, fourth (315); Mary Fechtig, fifth (323); and Lisa Chirichetti, seventh (324). Lynn Dennison finished twelfth, with 328. Each of IU's top five finishers advanced to the NCAA championship meet, but none managed to score in the top twenty.

Left to right: **Lisa Chirichetti, Tracy Chapman, Lynn Dennison, Michele Redman, Sarah DeKraay, Mary Fechtig**, and coach **Sam Carmichael**.

Sam Carmichael, a native of Martinsville, Indiana, became a golfer at an early age under the tutelage of his father, Don Carmichael, a golf pro at the Martinsville Country Club. During his collegiate golf career at Louisiana State, he was a member of the 1960 team that won both the Southern Intercollegiate and the Southeastern Conference championships. That same year, he won the Indiana State Junior and the Indiana State Amateur tourneys, and the Indiana State Open. His record four-round score of 266 in the latter still stands today. He turned professional in 1962.

Early in 1981, Carmichael was appointed head coach of the IU women's golf team. He soon helped turn the team into one of the best in the Big Ten; IU won the conference title in 1986, 1987, 1990, 1992, 1995, and 1996, and ended up in the runner-up spot in six years.

In 1991, Sam succeeded Bob Fitch as the men's golf coach, and the team captured the Big Ten championship, with medalist Shaun Micheel's 276 leading the way. The team's 1,138 strokes broke the four-round Big Ten record.

Carmichael was named Women's NCAA Coach of the Year in 1987; Women's Big Ten Coach of the Year in 1985, 1986, 1987, 1988, 1995, and 1996; and Men's Big Ten Coach of the Year in 1991.

Golfer **Sarah DeKraay** won the Big Ten championship in 1986, with a four-round total of 313, becoming IU's first conference medalist. She placed second in the tourney the following year. The year she won the Big Ten, DeKraay shot an IU record 68 at the Northern Invitational. She had a season average of 75.9 in 1987, and a four-year average of 77.3. She was All–Big Ten in 1985, 1986, and 1987, earning All-American honorable mention each of those years.

Golfer **Michele Redman** was All–Big Ten in each of her four years at IU. She had a career average of 77.5. She was a member of the Big Ten championship teams in 1986 and 1987, and was the Big Ten Tournament medalist in 1987. Redman earned honorable mention on the All-American team in 1986 and was named to the second team in 1987. She was the 1997 winner of the Ladies' PGA Big Apple Classic.

The 1990 women's golf team captured the Big Ten title at Minnesota with 1,232 strokes, topping second-place Iowa by 45. IU junior Shannon Hardesty won the tournament with a 290, 9 strokes better than the second-place finisher. Four other Hoosiers—Debbie Lee, Angela Buzminski, Jen Myers, and Amy McDonald—contributed to IU's scoring in the four rounds of tournament play. Lee was named the Big Ten Player of the Year. Team members Buzminski (1991, 1992, and 1993), Hardesty (1990 and 1991), and Lee (1989 and 1991) were All–Big Ten selections during their play at IU. McDonald finished second in the Big Ten Tournament in 1992, and Buzminski was second in both the Big Ten and NCAA tournaments in 1993.

Front row, left to right: **Debbie Lee, Shannon Hardesty, Lori Stinson, Courtney Cox, Amy McDonald**, and coach **Sam Carmichael**; back row: **Sue Soderberg, Angela Buzminski, Angie Mills, Jen Myers, Lindsay Munson**, and **Kris Kropechot**.

Shannon Hardesty was the medalist in the Big Ten golf championship in 1990, when she shot a four-round total of 298 to lead IU to its third Big Ten title. She was an All–Big Ten selectee in 1990 and 1991. She achieved her best three-round total, 219, at the Lady Buckeye Invitational in 1990.

Women's Gymnastics

ymnastics was a popular women's sport at IU for many years. It started as a club sport in the early 1910s, becoming a varsity sport in 1967/68. The home meets for the team were originally held in the Women's HPER Gymnasium, and admission was free. In 1969/70, the Department of Physical Education for Women allocated only $70 for the team. In 1984/85, in

Below: The 1974 women's gymnastics team. Front row, left to right: **Marsha Marshall, Pam Peiffer**, team captain **Becky Stoner, Lisa Farnsworth, Louise Denham**, and assistant coach **Dayna Daniels**; back row: **Sue Amberg, Krista Thomas, Louise Gerstung, Jackie Sanders, Jan Lehman**, and **Pat Markey**. **Charles Simpson**, who volunteered his services as coach, is at the far left.

contrast, the Athletic Department supported the team in the amount of $57,552. That was its final season, however, as women's gymnastics was discontinued as a varsity sport.

From 1968 through 1976, the team had four coaches: Emmelyn Wheeler, C. Bittermuer, Charles Simpson, and Carol Bain. Diane Schulz took over in 1976 and led the squad through its final season. Carol Weldon was a standout performer in the early years. In 1982, Kathy Rice and Sally Swain were outstanding performers on the parallel bars and the balance beam, respectively. Susie Lovell and Aimee Comparet provided excellent all-around talent. IU first participated in the Big Ten championship tourney in 1982, finishing fifth in a field of eight. That was the team's best tournament showing.

At the time women's gymnastics was discontinued as a varsity sport, twelve coeds were tendered athletes. During its last season, thirteen young women, five of them freshmen, were eligible to participate. Support was continued as long as the women were registered as full-time undergraduate students. Over its life span as a varsity sport, the IU gymnasts won 62 matches and lost 55. Currently, seven schools compete in women's gymnastics in the Big Ten: Iowa, Illinois, Michigan, Michigan State, Minnesota, Ohio State, and Penn State.

Carol Weldon is shown performing on the balance beam as a senior in 1978. She was one of five gymnasts to receive athletic scholarships in 1976/77, and was one of IU's leaders under Coach Diane Schulz.

Susie Lovell was one of the original tendered athletes in women's gymnastics in 1976/77. She was an outstanding all around performer.

Women's Tennis

Women students at Indiana University played intramural tennis as early as 1905, but it was sixty-two years before an IU coed tennis team competed against teams from other schools. In the fall of 1973, the women's team won over DePauw, Taylor, Ball State, and Eastern Kentucky, but lost to the University of Kentucky.

The glory days for IU's women's tennis began in 1980, three years after Ernest Linwood "Lin" Loring joined the coaching staff. The team has now dominated the Big Ten for well over a decade and a half. It led the Big Ten standings in 1980 and 1981. The first official Big Ten women's tennis championship tournament was held in Madison, Wisconsin, in 1982. Indiana won that championship, the first of fourteen; the team has finished second or third in the remaining meets. Since Loring arrived, the teams have lost only 19 matches in conference play; they had 104 consecutive victories against Big Ten opponents during an eight-year period.

Since 1982, seventeen Hoosier women have been named to the All-American team, and sixty to the All–Big Ten team. Four Hoosiers have been honored as the Big Ten Player of the Year: Kelly Mulvihill in 1988 and 1989, Deborah Edelman in 1990 and 1992, Stephanie Reece in 1991 and 1993, and Jody Yin in 1994. In 1982, Heather Crowe won both the 1982 AIAW singles title and the Broderick (Outstanding Female College Athlete) Award. Janet McCutcheon, a member of the class of 1987, was a two-time All–Big Ten player and a 1987 All-American.

Loring has coached many other outstanding players, including Kelly Ferguson, Bev Ramser, Tina McHall (the first African American tennis player at IU), Tracy Hoffman, Diane McCormick, Wendy Allen, Gretchen Doninger, Rachel Epstein, Natasha Joshi, Lizl Coetsee, Zahra Ahamed, Kelly Fitzgerald, Christy Sharp, and Rebbeca Wallihan.

Loring's teams have compiled an enviable record, the best record of any Indiana University coach in any sport:

485 wins and 110 losses, against all opponents, and 229 wins and only 17 losses (93.1%) in the Big Ten, with fourteen championship crowns. The team has had players in the NCAA competition every year since 1979, and in 1982 they won the NCAA crown. Loring has been named the Big Ten, Midwest, and National Coach of the Year; he has won three additional Big Ten awards, four more Midwest honors, and another national honor in 1992. In addition, the academic record of his teams is as impressive as their tennis record: every team member has completed her degree at IU.

Heather Crowe was a leader on the tennis team that won the 1982 NCAA title, and she was the NCAA singles champion that year. She is shown here receiving the Broderick Award, given to the nation's top woman college athlete. Crowe was an All-American in 1981 and 1982 and an All–Big Ten player in 1980, 1981, 1982, and 1983, leading IU to titles each of those years.

The 1988 women's tennis team went into the Big Ten tournament in Bloomington seeded number one, and proceeded to win their seventh consecutive championship. They defeated Iowa 9 to 0 in the first round, Michigan State 9 to 0 in the second, and Wisconsin 6 to 3 in the championship match. Reka Monoki, Candy Kopetzki, Gretchen Doninger, and Brenda Hacker were undefeated in their singles matches. Kopetzki and Cara Beth Lee and Shawn Foltz and Amy Alcini swept all of their doubles matches. Junior Kelly Mulvihill, sophomore Kopetzki, and senior Monoki were named to the All–Big Ten first team, and sophomore Foltz and freshman Doninger were second team selections. Mulvihill and Tina Basle of Michigan were named Big Ten Tennis Players of the Year. Coach Lin Loring was Co–Big Ten Coach of the Year.

Front row: **Shawn Foltz, Amy Alcini, Brenda Hacker, Kelly Mulvihill, Reka Monoki** (holding the trophy), **Gretchen Doninger**, and **Cara Beth Lee**; back row: assistant coach **Sonny Reddy**, assistant coach **Sue Hutchinson**, coach **Lin Loring**, and **Candy Kopetzki**.

Stephanie Reece, from Indianapolis, was a member of IU's eighth, ninth, and tenth Big Ten championship tennis teams. She was the Big Ten Freshman of the Year in 1989 and the Big Ten Player of the Year in 1991 and 1992 (tying with Debbie Edelman). She was an All–Big Ten player each of her four years at IU. Reece teamed with Kelly Mulvihill to win the All-American Doubles Championship in 1988. She was an All-American doubles player with Mulvihill in 1989, and with Debbie Edelman in 1990 and 1991, and an All-American singles winner in 1991 and 1992.

Deborah Edelman, a native of Oswego, Illinois, was the Big Ten Freshman of the Year and Big Ten Player of the Year in 1990. She tied for the latter honor with teammate and doubles partner Stephanie Reece in 1992. Debbie was a Big Ten all-star pick in each of her four years at IU. She was an All-American selection in doubles competition with Reece in 1991 and 1992 and with Rachel Epstein in 1993, and in singles competition in 1992.

Opposite: **Kelly Mulvihill** was the Big Ten Tennis Player of the Year in 1988 and 1989, and was an All–Big Ten player in 1987, 1988, and 1989. With Janet McCutcheon in 1987 and Stephanie Reece in 1989, she won All-American honors in the doubles competition. She and Reece were the All-American doubles champions in 1988.

(1968)
Women's Softball

IU coeds were playing some form of baseball as early as 1900. According to the March 16, 1918, issue of the *Indiana Daily Student,* "There are about 75 girls participating in baseball this year," from whom four teams were picked to compete for the school championship. Since practices were held in the Women's Gymnasium of the Student Building, it seems unlikely that a hard ball was used. The very early rules differed somewhat from the men's: the catcher was permitted to use a mitt; the ball was softer; smaller bats were used; the distances between bases were shorter; and the team had only seven fielding positions (neither a shortstop nor a centerfielder was listed in the lineup).

Women's intercollegiate softball began at Indiana in 1968, when a few games were played with other colleges in the state. Coached by Jenny Johnson and Louetta Bloecher, the early teams struggled, but IU had a winning record of 16 and 9 in 1977. The program proved to be popular with women athletes, and by 1979, Indiana's team had won national acclaim. Coached by Ann Lawver, the 1979 team had a record of 28 and 12. The players included pitcher/shortstop Donna Michalek, who was the winning pitcher in thirteen games while losing six, and who had an earned run average of 1.81 and a batting average of .405; left-handed first baseman Linda Spagnola, who batted .345; catcher Diane Stephenson, IU's current softball coach; infielder Jan Scholl; pitcher/catcher Ginger Gilles; and infielder and hockey player Sue Garnier. IU won the Big Ten, the Indiana AIAW, and the Midwest AIAW championships that year, and capped the season by winning three games and losing two in the double elimination meet of the National AIAW World Series. The IU women's softball team won the Big Ten championship again in 1980, 1983, 1986, and 1994. In 1986, they also won the NCAA Mideast Regional Championship, which put them in the NCAA Softball College World Series. The Hoosiers beat Louisiana Tech in the first round, but lost to Texas A&M, ending up in a third-place tie with the University of California. The Big Ten title that year was

Diane Stephenson was the first woman to receive a full scholarship as a student athlete at Indiana University. Her skills as a catcher earned her a spot on the 1981 All-American softball team. In her senior year she was the winning pitcher in ten of IU's victories, losing only two games. A power hitter, Stephenson also led the team in sacrifice bunts. She had 25 career doubles, 133 hits, and 77 runs batted in.

Stephenson became an assistant softball coach at IU in 1984, and then the head coach in 1988. Her record to date as the Hoosier coach is 301 wins, 211 losses, and 2 ties.

In 1983, **Terry Deluca** was named to the All-American softball team. She had been named to the All–Big Ten team the previous year. An outstanding outfielder with a strong and accurate arm, she was a key member of the 1983 Big Ten championship team. Deluca had 167 hits and scored 93 runs in her IU career. The 1983 team posted a record of 45 wins, 20 losses and 1 tie. They advanced to the NCAA regionals, but lost their first game in the NCAA College World Series.

the third under the leadership of coach Gayle Blevins. The team was led by seniors: outfielder Karleen Moore, shortstop Pam Lee, and pitcher/first baseman Amy Unterbrink. The first two titles came as the result of unofficial tournament play. In addition to AIAW post-season play, the IU softball team has been selected to compete in NCAA post-season play five times: 1983, 1985, 1986, 1994, and 1996.

From 1974 through 1996, the team won 665 and lost 420 against all opponents, for a 61.3 winning percentage; their Big Ten record was 178 and 138. During a single spring softball season, the team competes in as many as 63 games, playing a large number of double-headers on weekends and during spring break.

Five of IU's softball players have been named to the women's All-American softball team: catcher Diane Stephenson (1981), outfielder Terry Deluca (1882), outfielder Linda Thaler (1984), outfielder Karleen Moore (1986), and pitcher Amy Unterbrink (1986). The 1994 Big Ten Player of the Year was IU's Michelle Venturella, who was also an alternate on the 1996 U.S. Olympic softball team. Other outstanding players have been Deb

Linda Thaler was named to the All-American softball team and to the All–Big Ten team as an outstanding outfielder in 1984. She was an excellent bunter but could also hit the long ball, and she had good speed on the base paths. During her IU career (1981–1984), she hit 27 doubles and 18 triples, and stole 26 bases. Her slugging percentage in 1982 was .540.

Karleen Moore, shown here with Coach **Gayle Blevins**, was a transfer from the University of Colorado. She was selected to the All-American Softball Team in 1986, was on the All–Big Ten team in 1985 and 1986, and was an Academic All-American in 1986 and 1987. She was awarded the Big Ten Medal of Honor in 1987. Moore was a fine centerfielder and an excellent bunter and base runner. She had a batting average of .362 in 657 at-bats. She had 283 hits, scored 119 runs, and leads all IU women softballers with 83 stolen bases. She helped bring a Big Ten title to IU in 1986.

Hockemeyer (1976), infielder Brenda Thaler (1981–1984), pitcher Christy Brown (1987–1990), Marji Ledgerwood (1977–1990), outfielder Candace Nishina (1991–1994), outfielder Margaret Haenisch (1991–1994), third baseman/shortstop Aimee Lonigro (1994–1996), pitcher Gina Ugo (1993–1996), and shortstop/third baseman Monica Armendarez (1995–1997). Since 1985, twenty-three Indiana softballers have been selected by the coaches to the All–Big Ten first team.

The Indiana softball team has had five coaches since 1973: Jenny Johnson (1973–1974), Louetta Bloecher (1975–1976), Ann Lawver (1977–1979), Gayle Blevins (1980–1987), and Diane Stephenson (1988–). Lawver's team won the inaugural Big Ten tourney, and Blevins's won the second. Blevins was selected Coach of the Year in 1986; Stephenson was Regional Coach of the Year and Big Ten Coach of the Year in 1994. The Indiana University varsity softball diamond, constructed in 1975, is located behind Foster Quadrangle adjacent to Sembower Field. It has a well-maintained brick dust base infield surface and a natural grass outfield surface. The outfield fences are 190 feet at the left and right field foul poles and 220 feet in centerfield from home plate, and there is a 15-foot warning track in front of the outfield fence. The facility has covered dugouts, a press box, and bleachers that can seat approximately 1,000 spectators. Batting cages and locker room space are located in the nearby Gladstein Fieldhouse.

In 1986, 6'1" senior **Amy Unterbrink** led the Hoosiers to a Big Ten title in softball and a third-place finish in the NCAA College World Series. She established the Big Ten record for the lowest ERA, with 0.21 earned runs per game in 133 innings pitched. During her three-year career at IU, Unterbrink struck out a total of 358 batters in 357²/₃ innings. She had 26 shutouts and 3 no-hitters, pitching two perfect games in 1986. She was an All-American pitcher in 1986, and was a three-time All–Big Ten selection.

Shirley Bryant played basketball at IU from 1992 to 1995. She led the team in rebounding, scoring, and field goal shooting percentage during each of her four years of play; her career field goal shooting percentage was .586, with 627 goals in 1,070 attempts. She had 22 rebounds in a game against Michigan in 1995. The 5'10" senior from Lexington, Kentucky, was co-captain of the team during her senior year of play at IU. She was the Sports Channel Big Ten Freshman of the Year in 1992 and was named to the All–Big Ten second team in 1995.

Lisa Furlin had a 3-point field goal shooting percentage of .488 during the 1994/95 season, to lead all Lady Hoosiers. In 1993 she shot .904 from the free throw line, hitting 12 out of 12 in a game against Wisconsin; her career free throw percentage was .821. She accumulated a total of 1,451 points, scoring more than 30 points in a game on four occasions. She led the team in scoring in 1996 with 394 points. Furlin was on the Sports Channel All–Big Ten Freshman Team in 1993 and was the Varsity Club Scholar Athlete of the Year in 1995.

The 6'5" **Quacy Barnes**, a native of Benton Harbor, Michigan, was an excellent center for IU. "Q" led the Lady Hoosiers in blocked shots during her first three seasons. She led the team in rebounding, scoring, and field goal percentage in 1997. Barnes was on the Academic All–Big Ten team in 1996, and she was a member of the Big Ten Conference All-Star team that toured Scandinavia.

In 1995, Katie Weismiller's third year as coach, the women's volleyball team had a record of 20 wins and 14 losses. They won the Monon Spike Match and tied for fourth place in the Big Ten with a record of 12 and 8, before advancing to the NCAA tournament and falling to George Mason.

The team is pictured here at the Sample Gates. Bottom row, left to right: **Demetra Marcus, Bonnie Ludlow, Melissa Brawner, Stephanie Goehl, Marcee Prothro, Julie Flatley, Lindsay Trudell, Jen Sutton**, and **Tanya Marchiol**; top row: **Stacie Murr, Michelle McElroy, Heather Magelssen, Melissa Rooney, Jen Magelssen, Jen Manghan**, and **Emily Bodger**.

Michelle McElroy, who played volleyball for Indiana from 1991 to 1995, is the school record holder in assists, with a total of 4,294, and ranks sixth in digs, with 882. She was an Academic All–Big Ten player in 1994 and 1995, and received All–Big Ten honorable mention in 1995.

Julie Flatley, a 5'11" member of the IU women's volleyball team, was an outstanding outside hitter throughout her career. The native of St. Louis earned All–Big Ten honors as a sophomore in 1995. On September 29, 1997, Flatley was named both National and Big Ten Player of the Week. She was selected to the All-District team. She led the team in 1997 with 426 kills, 226 dogs, and 103 blocks.

The IU women golfers won their second consecutive Big Ten title in 1996. The tournament, held at the IU course, was shortened to 54 holes because of heavy rain. IU beat out second-place Ohio State by 21 strokes (946 to 967). Erika Wicoff's final round of 75 gave her a total of 226, 6 strokes better than her teammate Stacy Quilling, who was the runner-up. Mary Vajgrt shot 245, Jenny Gray 246, Erin Carney 248, and Jennifer Seger 249. The team participated in seven invitationals in addition to the Big Ten meet, finishing first in four of them: the Lady Buckeye, the Top Flite/Peggy Kir Bell, the Lady Northern, and the Minnesota Invitational.

Front row, left to right: **Erin Carney, Erika Wicoff, Stacy Quilling**, and **Jenny Gray**; back row: **Kimberly Hsu, Jennifer Seger, Brandy Ferdinand, Mary Vajgrt**, and coach **Sam Carmichael**.

Erika Wicoff, a native of Hartford City, Indiana, won three Big Ten women's golf championships and was a three-time All–Big Ten first team selectee (1994–1996). Wicoff was the Big Ten Freshman of the Year in 1993. She was a first team All-American in 1995 and 1996. At the NCAA East Regional in 1994, she fired a 69 in one round; she had a four-round low of 288 at the NCAA Championships in 1995. Wicoff had an average of 76.1 strokes per 18 holes during her four years of play at IU. In 1997 she tied for 8th, after a final round of 66, at the Nashville LPGA Sara Lee Classic.

The 1982 women's tennis team won the Big Ten championship by defeating Illinois 9 to 0, Michigan State 9 to 0, and Northwestern 8 to 1 in the title match. The team had a 15 and 0 record in dual matches with all Big Ten opponents. Lin Loring's squad went on to win the Midwest Regional title and the NCAA championships.

The IU women had an overall record of 37 wins and only 1 loss (to South Carolina, by a score of 4 to 5). Indiana placed third in the South Carolina Invitational, and won the Michigan State, Nike, and Clemson invitational tourneys.

During the Big Ten season, Heather Crowe won 22 matches and lost 2, Tracy Hoffman was 24 and 1, Jenny Snyder went 19 and 3, Bev Ramser won 10 and lost 1, and Diane McCormick was 15 and 2. In the National Tennis Finals at Iowa City, IU defeated Iowa (9 to 0), North Carolina (8 to 1), and Texas (5 to 4) before beating Cal Berkeley in the finals by a score of 6 to 3. Heather Crowe won the singles competition, and she and Tracy Hoffman received All-American honors. Coach Loring was named Coach of the Year.

Front row, left to right: **Bev Ramser, Tracy Hoffman, Heather Crowe**, and assistant coach **Nancy Stevenson**; back row: **Marianne Guiney, Jenny Snyder, Anne Hutchens, Diane McCormick**, and coach **Lin Loring**.

Rachel Epstein won Big Ten tennis honors in 1993, 1994, and 1995, and was highly instrumental in IU's winning the Big Ten titles during each of those years. She was an All-American in 1993, when she teamed with Debbie Edelman in the doubles.

Tennis star Jody Yin was the Big Ten Freshman of the Year in 1991, and the Big Ten Player of the Year in 1994. She won All–Big Ten honors in 1991, 1992, 1993, and 1994. She was a key player on IU's 10th, 11th, 12th, and 13th Big Ten championship teams.

The 1994 softball team won the Big Ten championship with a conference record of 23 wins and 5 losses, then advanced to the NCAA Mideast Regionals, finishing second. The team was led by catcher Michelle Venturella, pitcher Gina Ugo, third baseman Karen Kron, shortstop Aimee Lonigro, outfielder Candace Nishina, and designated player Meg Montgomery. Kron was named the team's Most Valuable Defensive Player; she was an Academic All–Big Ten selection, and as a junior was the recipient of the Anita Aldrich Award, presented to IU's top female scholar athlete. Nishina was selected to the All–Big Ten team along with Ugo and Venturella.

Front row, left to right: assistant coach **Terry Knecht, Jenn Holloway, Margaret Haenisch, Jannette Campbell, Misten Mager, Angie Rapp, Kara Manley, Aimee Lonigro, Jenny Mitchell, Candace Nishina**, and coach **Diane Stephenson**; back row: manager **Sarah Haynes, Karen Kron, Kellie Brandt, Meg Montgomery, Kassey Reynolds, Gina Ugo, Michelle Venturella**, and assistant coach **Sally Miller**.

Gina Ugo was a star softball pitcher for IU. In 1996 she led the Big Ten in games pitched (23), complete games pitched (20), innings pitched (157), and games won (16), and struck out 127 batters. She had a career earned run average of 1.16. Ugo was named Big Ten Pitcher of the Year in 1996 and was a three-time All–Big Ten selection (1994–96). She was named to the All-American third team for her play during her senior year at IU. She was awarded the Big Ten Medal of Honor in 1996.

Michelle Venturella was an outstanding all-around softball player and catcher. In 1994 she set the Big Ten records for most total bases (69) and most runs batted in (33) in a season. Her .486 was the second-highest batting average in the Big Ten, and she is third in the NCAA record book with 56 walks in 65 games the same year. She was voted 1994 Player of the Year. Michelle was a second team All-American in 1994 and an All–Big Ten catcher in 1994 and 1995. She won the Big Ten Medal of Honor in 1995.

Monica Armendarez, an outstanding shortstop on the Hoosier softball team, set a school record with her .427 batting average in 1997. She led the team in many batting statistics, was an All–Big Ten player, and was a second team All-American her junior year. In 1998 she topped the home run record formerly held by Michelle Venturella.

Kimiko Hirai, from Longmont, Colorado, is one of the university's recent star divers. She transferred to IU from Colorado State in 1995. In 1996, Hirai placed second in the Big Ten three meter springboard competition and won the NCAA one meter diving championship; she was named Diver of the Year. She shared Indiana's Female Athlete of the Year award with golfer Erika Wicoff that year. A shoulder injury and two separate surgical repairs prevented her participation in the 1997 season. She hopes to compete in the 2000 Olympics. In 1997, the National Association of Collegiate Directors of Athletics selected Hirai as one of ten recipients of a $5,000 scholarship grant to be used toward postgraduate studies.

As a prep star in Bloomfield Hills, Michigan, **Jennifer Dixon** was a four-time All-American. As a college freshman, she placed third in the one meter event at the Big Ten meet. She was runner-up in the one meter platform dive at the U.S. Olympic Festival in 1994. In 1995, Dixon won the Big Ten one meter dive, finishing third in the platform and fifth in the three meter. IU's only representative to the NCAA, she finished out of the running, but was named to the All-American squad. She was redshirted because of injuries in 1996 and was Academic All–Big Ten. Dixon was named Big Ten Diver of the Year in 1997 after winning both the one and the three meter events at the Big Ten Championships.

Jerry Yeagley joined the faculty of IU's School of HPER in 1963 and became the coach of the Hoosier Soccer Club. He took over as coach of the university team when soccer became a varsity sport in 1973. He has been the architect of the premier college soccer program in the United States. Yeagley strongly believes in "player development," accepting walk-ons who show promise. His teams have appeared in 22 NCAA Tournaments and made 11 Final Four appearances; they have won more NCAA Tourney games (45) than any other college team in the U.S., and established a Big Ten record unbeaten streak of 68 games. His first NCAA title win, 2 to 1 over Duke in 1982, was the second-longest college soccer game in history, at 2 hours and 39 minutes.

Brian Maisonneuve was an All–Big Ten player in 1991, 1992, 1993, and 1994, and was the conference MVP in 1993 and 1994. He helped lead the Hoosiers to Big Ten championships in 1991, 1992, and 1994. He had 54 goals, 22 assists, and 110 points during his career, which ranks him at the top of the Big Ten. He was an All-American his last two seasons and received the Hermann Trophy his senior year. He was a U.S. Olympian in 1996. Maisonneuve received the Gimbel Award in 1995.

Todd Yeagley was a standout player for his coach and father, Jerry Yeagley, during his four years (1991–94) as a Hoosier. A four-time All–Big Ten player, he is second on IU's all-time list in assists. One of the most versatile soccer players at IU, Yeagley was a steadying force on the team, which had a record of 71 victories, 15 losses, and 7 ties during his career. He was a second team All-American during his first three years and a first team All-American his senior year. He was the Missouri Athletic Club Player of the Year and the Soccer American Player of the Year in 1994.

Scott Coufal was one of IU's great goalkeepers during his college career (1993–1996). Playing with such teammates as Chris Klein, Brian Maisonneuve, Caleb Porter, Harry Weiss, and Todd Yeagley, he participated in 88 games, with a record of 66 wins, 14 losses, and 6 ties. Coufal had a total of 274 saves in his career; he leads all IU goalkeepers with 38 shutouts and 66 wins. His career goals-against-average (GAA) was 0.65; he ranked second in the nation with a GAA of 0.53 in 1994. In four NCAA tournaments, he allowed only seven goals in eleven games. Coufal was Soccer America's Freshman Goalkeeper of the Year in 1993 and an All–Big Ten Player in 1994 and 1996. In his senior year he was a finalist for the Hermann Trophy Award and the MAC Player of the Year Award.

Some of the members of the 1997 men's soccer team celebrate and show off the Big Ten championship trophy follow-ing their 1 to 0 victory over Ohio State in the tournament finals. From left to right: **Simon Deery**, co-captains **Caleb Porter** and **Chris Klein**, Tony Cerroni, Ben Londergan, Justin Tauber, and **Yuri Lavrinenko**.

The two track and cross country coaches, **Roseann Barnhill Wilson** and **Sam Bell**, enjoy a light moment at a women's indoor track meet in 1997.

Hilary Bruening, a middle-distance runner, won the Big Ten 600 meter run in 1995 and the Big Ten indoor and outdoor 800 meter run in 1997. She set the Hoosiers' best indoor 800 meter time with a clocking of 2:14.50. As a result of her fine performances, Bruening was named to the U.S. World University team in 1997. She was IU's Female Athlete of the Year for 1996/97.

The 1996 women's soccer team won the Big Ten Tournament, shutting out their opponents in three games. The men won their fifth Big Ten title in six years. Athletic director **Clarence Doninger** is shown here displaying the men's trophy; **Kathy Kozar** holds the women's trophy. Others shown are, left to right: **Caleb Porter** of the men's team and **Kris Fosdick, Carrie Watts**, and **Jennifer Cartwell**.

The women went into the NCAA Tournament with an overall record of 11 and 11, and a Big Ten record of 2 and 5. They lost to Notre Dame in the first round. The men had a season record of 12 wins, 2 losses, and 2 ties going into the Big Ten Tournament. They won the championship and entered the NCAA playoffs for the 21st time in 24 years. They defeated Evansville and Bowling Green before losing to Florida International in a quarterfinal match.

Wendy Dillinger, a native of St. Charles, Missouri, was a four-time Prep All-Conference player. An outstanding offensive player, she was an All–Big Ten midfielder in 1994, and played in all of IU's games in 1995. She was redshirted in 1996, because she had an appendectomy immediately prior to the start of the season. Dillinger is the leading scorer in the short history of IU women's soccer, with a total of 72 points. She holds a total of ten IU records.

Merit Elzey was a Parade All-American in 1994 as a prep, then went on to be an outstanding goalkeeper for the Hoosier women's soccer team. She had a remarkable three shutouts in the 1996 Big Ten Tournament. During her first three years at IU, Elzey started every game at goal. In 1995 she was named the All-Region and All–Big Ten goalie, and in her junior year she earned All-Region and All–Big Ten second team honors.

Tracy Grose was a superb forward on the Hoosier women's soccer team. In 1995 she was named the Big Ten Freshman of the Year and a second team All–Big Ten winner. She led the team in scoring that year, with 17 points. She was redshirted in 1996, because of a torn anterior cruciate ligament prior to the start of the season.

Quincy Wolkowitz was a midfielder from St. Louis who joined the Hoosier soccer team in 1993. She started every game during her four-year career at IU, scoring 31 points, which ranks her third in that category. She was an Academic All–Big Ten player for three years.

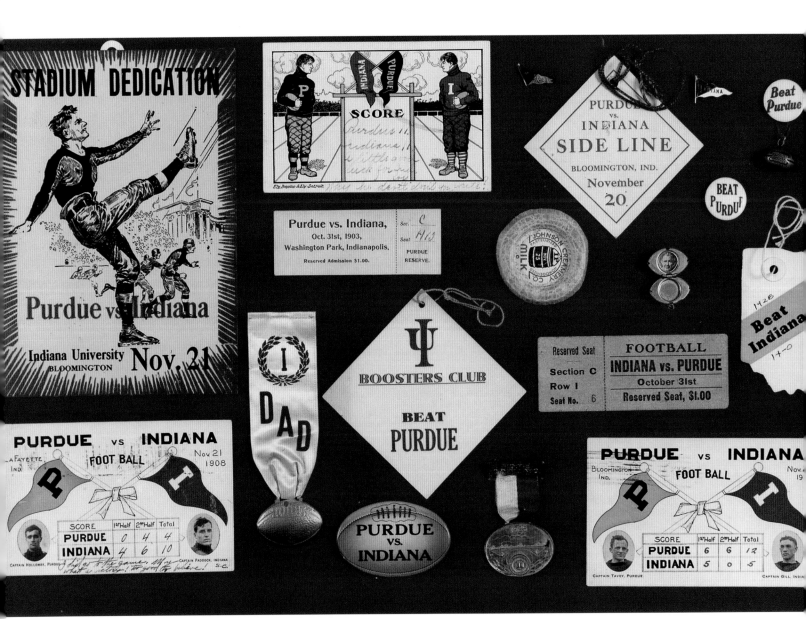

Football games between Indiana and Purdue were marked by the sale of signs, medals, buttons, brooches, and pins. The announcement of the dedication of the stadium, and the introduction of the Old Oaken Bucket are depicted here. The game against Purdue ended in a scoreless tie. From the Collection of John Pfeifer.

Badges, posters, helmets, shoes, pennants, pictures of the 1941 track team and the 1894 football team, Don Heistand's IU football blanket, an "I" sweater, and the *Chicago Tribune* Silver Football presented to Vern Huffman in 1936 are shown here. From the Collection of John Pfeifer, The University Archives, and Mrs. Vern Huffman.

FOOT BALL

INDIANA MEMORIAL STADIUM

NOV 4 DEDICATION

PURDUE VS. INDIANA — BLOOMINGTON

INDIANA

INDIANA ATHLETIC REVIEW
25 CENTS   SATURDAY - - OCT. 29, 1932   25 CENTS

MISS. STATE at INDIANA

Get Your I On The BUCKET

Don Heistand Football

Memorial Stadium was packed for this game against Ohio State in 1986. OSU beat Indiana 24 to 22. Assembly Hall and the Tennis Facility can be seen in the background.

Assembly Hall has been filled to capacity for nearly every home game. Here the Hoosiers and the Illini get ready to tip off in a 1996 game on the Branch McCracken Memorial Basketball Floor.

Women's Swimming and Diving

Swimming was part of the Women's Athletic Association program at IU as early as 1914. (According to the *Arbutus,* however, "Owing to a water shortage during the Fall Term, the girls were disappointed in not being able to use the swimming pool.") In 1936, the Department of Physical Education for Women sponsored the first intercollegiate meet for IU swimmers and divers; Indiana placed second against teams from colleges within the state. In March of that year, the coed swimmers competed against forty-four other teams in a national meet in Detroit sponsored by Wayne University (now Wayne State). The Hoosier team, which placed fifth, consisted of Barbara Tompkins, Virginia Warren, Barbara Deniston, Gretchen Hopman, and Helen Holmes. This aquatic division of women's sports was known as the Oceanides.

Jennifer Hooker, a native of Bloomington, holds the IU record in three freestyle events: 200 yards (1980), 500 yards (1981), and 1,650 yards (1981). She was an All-American in the 100, 200, and 500 yard freestyle in 1980, and in the 500 and 1,650 yard freestyle in 1981, and was a member of the 1981 All-American 400 yard freestyle relay team. She finished sixth in the 200 meter freestyle at the 1976 Olympics.

Hooker graduated from IU in 1984. She earned a JD degree from Vanderbilt in 1990, and later practiced law in St. Louis and Rochester, Minnesota. She returned to IU, earning her MS in kinesiology in 1996, while serving as an assistant to the director of the Athletic Department.

BIG TEN CHAMP

JENNIFER HOOKER
1650, 500, 200 FREE

Kate McDonald was a Big Ten Championship Individual Award winner in 1987. She was a prominent member of the IU women's swimming squads from 1985 to 1988. As a freshman, she teamed with Kelly Artz, Rosalie Wicht, and Vilma Aguilera to win the Big Ten 200 yard medley relay race. McDonald won Big Ten championships in the 100 yard backstroke in 1986 and 1987 and in the 100 yard freestyle in 1987 and 1988. She owns the Indiana record in both the 50 and 100 yard freestyle and the 100 yard backstroke events.

From 1993 to 1996, **Beth Burke** was a key member of the IU women's swim team. She excelled at the breaststroke and in the individual medley, and also competed in the butterfly and backstroke events. Burke holds the IU records in the 100 and 200 meter breaststroke swims. She was an Academic All–Big Ten swimmer in 1994 and 1995.

The 1969 season, the first for the Indiana women swimmers, was a successful one: IU won all seven of its meets, finishing fourth at the Nationals. The team won the unofficial Big Ten championships in 1971, 1972, and 1980. Thirty-five of its athletes have been named first team All-Americans, seventeen in diving and eighteen in swimming. Jennifer Hooker, Kate McDonald, and Beth Burke have held IU records in several swimming events. Jennifer Brooks was an outstanding recent butterfly and medley swimmer.

The swim team has had seven coaches since 1975: Don Glass (1975), Pat Barry (1979), Terry Townsend (1981), Bob Bruce (1982), Chet Jastremski (1986), Jill Sterkel (1991), and the current coach, Nancy Nitardy, IU's 1977 Big Ten butterfly champion, who took over in 1992. Her swimmers have won 20 meets while losing 27.

Hobie Billingsley coached the women's diving team from 1968 to 1989. His divers won five individual NCAA championships and four Big Ten crowns. Outstanding IU divers have included Leslie Bush, Cynthia Potter, Amy McGrath, Kristen Kane, and Kimiko Hirai. Bush was the Olympic ten meter gold medalist in 1964 and was inducted into the International Hall of Fame in 1986. Potter appeared in four Olympics and won a bronze medal in the three meter event in 1976; she is also a member of the International Hall of Fame. McGrath was an All-American diver in 1980, 1981, and 1982. Kane was the one meter and three meter All-American diver for four consecutive years (1991–1994). Hirai was the 1996 NCAA champion and Diver of the Year. Jennifer Dixon, earned All-American honors in 1995.

Leslie Bush was a two-time Olympian, winning the gold medal in the ten meter diving event in 1964. At the 1966 Student World Games (currently called the University World Games), she won the ten meter platform crown and placed second in the three meter springboard event. The following year she won the platform crown at the Pan-American Games. In addition, she won five national AAU diving championships. In June 1997, Bush was finally awarded an "I" for her athletic endeavors at IU in the 1960s.

Bush earned her BA in biology and a teaching certificate from IU in 1970. She has been a high school biology teacher for the last twenty-three years. Her teaching career started at the University of Arizona, where she was an unpaid diving coach. She was later the head coach for the men's and women's diving teams at Princeton University for two years.

Bush was elected to the International Swimming Hall of Fame in 1986. In 1987 she was the first woman to be elected to the IU Athletic Hall of Fame. She was awarded IU's Silver Anniversary award in 1995.

As a member of the U.S. Olympic diving team, **Cynthia Potter** competed twice in the ten meter event and twice in the three meter event. In 1971 she participated in the World Games, winning the three meter competition and finishing second in the ten meter event. She won a bronze medal at the 1975 Pan American Games and a silver medal at the 1978 World Championships. At the 1976 Olympics, she won the bronze medal in the three meter dive. She was the Big Ten one meter and three meter diving champion in 1972.

Potter coached both the men's and women's diving teams at Southern Methodist University from 1981 to 1984, then served as the men's and women's diving coach at the University of Arizona for five years. She now works as a TV sportscaster in Atlanta. In 1997 she received one of the NCAA Silver Anniversary awards, given to athletes who have distinguished themselves in the 25 years since completing their varsity careers. She was one of the ninety IU women athletes who returned to Bloomington in June 1997 to receive their "I" letters.

Kristen Kane was a four-time All-American diver at IU. She won the U.S. outdoor one meter diving championship in 1992 and the Big Ten three meter diving championship in 1992 and 1994. She was named Diver of the Year in 1992, 1993, and 1994. She was IU's Female Athlete of the Year in 1994.

Men's Soccer

A soccer club, consisting mostly of foreign students, was formed at IU in 1949. Gottfried K. "Joe" Guennel served as the coach: he remained in the position until 1960. Guennel was the person primarily responsible for promoting the game and its popularity in Indiana and the Midwest. The club's play was supported by a number of makeshift organizations and many individuals on the campus. The team was part of the Midwest Collegiate Soccer Conference, winning the conference championship in 1955, placing second in 1958, and sharing the title in 1959. Tom Morrell was a first team All-American selection in 1952, followed by Gus Omary in 1954, John Hicks and Joe Singer in 1955, and Ilan Rothmuller in 1958. Umit Kesim, Karl Schmidt, and Bob Nelson were named first team All-Americans in 1966, 1967, and 1972, respectively. The Joe Guennel Award is now presented to the most valuable senior player on the varsity soccer squad.

IU men's soccer entered the varsity arena in 1973, under the guidance of Jerry Yeagley, who took over as coach in 1963 and still remains at the helm. During that first season, the team compiled a record of 12 wins and 2 losses. With their high caliber of play, the Indiana soccer team quickly made their presence felt on the national scene. In the last twenty-five years, the Hoosiers have

Steve Burks played on Coach Jerry Yeagley's first varsity team in 1973. He was a four-year starter (1973–1976). He scored six goals against Indiana State in 1973, and five goals against Cincinnati in 1975. During his career, Burks scored 77 goals and had 28 assists, for a total of 182 points, a record he held until in 1990. He took more shots (345) than any other Hoosier. In his senior year, Burks earned All-American honors

In 1978, **Angelo DiBernardo** won the Hermann Trophy. He was the first IU player to receive this award, which is given each year to the nation's most outstanding college soccer player. DiBernardo played for Coach Yeagley from 1976 to 1978. He was a two-time (1977–78) All-American and played on the U.S. Olympic soccer team in 1980 and 1984. He scored 5 goals against St. Louis in 1976, and had 10 points and 4 assists against Dayton in 1976. He was one of IU's top five scorers, with 125 points. In both the 1976 and 1978 seasons, he scored 45 points.

made twenty-two NCAA Tournament appearances; they have appeared in eleven NCAA Final Four games since 1976, and have played in the NCAA finals eight times. They have won the NCAA title on three occasions (1982, 1983, 1988).

In 1982, IU was not scored on in the first three games of the NCAA Championships. In the finals, the team took an early lead over Duke, which tied the score in the second period to put the game into overtime. In the eighth overtime period, senior Greg Thompson scored his second goal of the game, to give the Hoosiers their first NCAA championship. Coach Yeagley became the first person to have both played on and coached an NCAA championship team.

IU's soccer matches were held in Memorial Stadium until 1981. In April of 1980, a plan was drawn up for the

John Putna was one of IU's early soccer stars. From 1976 to 1979, he played with such illustrious teammates as Armando Betancourt, Steve Burks, Angelo DiBernardo, Mike Freitag, Rudy Glenn, and Robert Meschbach. An outstanding goalkeeper, Putna had 112 saves in 1978 and led the IU defense to 14 shutouts and 23 wins. He permitted the fewest goals, 6, and had a goals-against-average (GAA) of 0.26 in 1979. His career GAA was 0.42. He had a total of 36 shutouts.

During **Armando Betancourt**'s three-year career at IU (1979–1981), the native Honduran scored 64 goals, 165 points, and 37 assists. He had 6 goals in the four-game NCAA championship tourney in 1980, when IU finished second behind San Francisco. Betancourt earned All-American honors in each of his three years of play at IU. He won the Hermann Trophy in 1981 as the collegiate soccer player of the year. He was honored as Collegiate Player of the Decade for the 1980s.

John Stollmeyer entered IU in January of 1982 as the Outstanding Amateur Soccer Player in the Nation. After helping lead the Hoosiers to their first NCAA championship the following fall, he was named the Outstanding Defensive Player, and was the first freshman player at Indiana to earn All-American status. The following year, he helped IU to another NCAA title. The 1984 team went back to the NCAA finals, but lost to Clemson by a score of 2 to 1; Stollmeyer was named again to the All-American team. In his senior season, Stollmeyer scored 27 points, including a team-leading 9 assists, but the team failed to reach the Final Four (losing in the regional final). He had 39 career assists. He was a durable player who started in all 99 games during his four-year IU career. He was given the Gimbel Award for his play and mental attitude.

construction of a new stadium for soccer and the Little 500. Estimated to cost $1.7 million, it would seat 25,000, and would be placed adjacent to the Billy Hayes Track. The new soccer field was inaugurated on September 13, 1981, when the Hoosiers played the 1980 NCAA champion, the University of San Francisco; IU won in overtime by a score of 2 to 1. The first Little 500 was held on the stadium track on April 24, 1982. On April 22, 1983, the facility was dedicated and named the William S. Armstrong Stadium.

In 1991, the Big Ten Conference added soccer to its list of varsity sports. Penn State had been playing soccer since 1911, Michigan State since 1953, Ohio State since 1956, Wisconsin since 1978, and Northwestern since 1980. Currently six Big Ten schools compete in this sport. IU has won or shared the Big Ten title in six of the seven years of conference play: the Hoosiers won in 1991, 1992, 1994, 1996, and 1997, and tied Wisconsin in 1995.

Coach Yeagley's teams play one of the most demanding schedules in the nation. Yeagley organizes a four-team classic in the early fall, inviting the top-rated college teams in the country to participate. His Cream and Crimson varsity team won its 400th victory on September 29, 1996, 2 to 1 over Michigan State. The team won eight more matches in 1996, giving him a record of 408 wins, 76 losses, and 36 ties, for a winning percentage of 78.5. Indiana has won more soccer games than any other school

Eight veterans of IU's two NCAA championship teams pose in the Well House with the two trophies they helped to earn. Front row, left to right: **Mike Hylla, Dan King**, and **Iker Zubizerreta**; back row: **Manuel Gorrity, Mark Laxgang, Dave Boncet, Keith Meyer**, and **Paul DiBernardo**. John Stollmeyer was not available for the photograph.

The 1983 squad had seventeen lettermen returning from the 1982 championship team. Paul DiBernardo, Manuel Gorrity, Mike Hylla, Greg Kennedy, Mark Laxgang, Pat McGauley, Chris Peterson, John Stollmeyer, and Iker Zubizerreta were once again the best of the Big Ten. The Hoosiers lost the first game of the season to Penn State, then had a seventeen-game winning streak going into the NCAA tourney. In the first game of the tournament, against Akron, IU took the lead on a first-half goal by Paul DiBernardo. The match went into overtime and was won by IU on a goal by Mike Hylla. With goals by Iker Zubizerreta and Mark Laxgang, the Hoosiers defeated St. Louis; two goals by Laxgang and one by DiBernardo against Virginia put Indiana in the championship game. IU downed previously undefeated and untied Columbia 1 to 0 on Paul McGauley's overtime goal, giving Indiana back-to-back NCAA championships. McGauley was named the tournament's Most Valuable Player.

Opposite: The IU men's soccer team was ranked number two in the 1988 pre-season polls, but after impressive victories over highly ranked teams, the Hoosiers moved into the number one position. They had a 15–3–3 record going into the NCAA tournament, in which all of their games would be played in Armstrong Stadium. After a first-round bye, IU defeated Boston by a score of 3 to 1 on goals by Michael Correia, Simon Katner, and Ken Snow. Seton Hall was next, and goals by Sean Shapert, Jim Crockford, and Correia gave the Hoosiers another 3 to 1 victory. In the semifinals, IU topped Portland 1 to 0 on a goal by Katner late in the first half. In the championship game against Howard, Sean Shapert scored the only goal of the first half; goalkeepers Juergen Sommer and Matt Olson turned away every Howard scoring threat to secure the crown.

The 1988 team was led by the outstanding play of Ken Snow, MAC Player of the Year and the Hermann Trophy winner. Snow, who scored 18 goals that season, was aided by the offensive play of Herb Behringer, Correia, Crockford, Herb Haller, Katner, Wes Priest, Han Roest, Shapert, and Ted Tsandes, and by the superb goaltending of Sommer and Olson, who had fourteen shutouts.

Pete Stoyanovich played for Coach Yeagley's soccer teams from 1985 to 1987. He had 9 goals and 4 assists in the 1985 season and tallied a total of 23 goals. He was also an outstanding place-kicker for Coach Bill Mallory's football squad. Stoyanovich has had a highly successful career in professional football as a place-kicker for the Miami Dolphins and the Kansas City Chiefs.

in the nation during Yeagley's career with the Hoosiers. In 1996, the Big Red soccer men advanced once again to the NCAA tournament, where they eventually were defeated in the quarter-final round.

IU soccer players have been selected to the All–Big Ten first team on twenty-four occasions; midfielder Brian Maisonneuve was honored as Big Ten Player of the Year in 1993 and 1994. Angelo DiBernardo, Ken Snow (twice), Armando Betancourt, and Maisonneuve have won the Hermann Trophy, and Todd Yeagley and Snow (twice) have been awarded the Missouri Athletic Club Award (the equivalent of the New York Athletic Club's Heisman Trophy). Juergen Sommer was named the Adidas Goal-

Ken Snow, the nation's leading scorer in 1988, with the help of assist leader Sean Shapert and goalkeeper Juergen Sommer, helped lead the Hoosiers to their third NCAA championship. As a freshman, Snow led the nation in scoring with 28 goals and 5 assists. In both 1988 and 1990, he was awarded the Hermann Trophy as Collegiate Player of the Year (voted by the soccer coaches and media nationwide) and was named the Missouri Athletic Club Player of the Year (which recognizes the best U.S. collegiate soccer player and is equivalent to football's Heisman Trophy). He was an All-American in 1987, 1988, 1989, and 1990. Snow leads all IU scorers with 84 goals and 196 points, and had 28 assists in his career.

keeper of the Year in 1990. Steve Burks, Tom Redman, John Putna, Mike Freitag, Robert Meschbach, Paul DiBernardo, John Stollmeyer, Sean Shapert, Greg Thompson, Pete Stoyanovich, and Juergen Sommer have helped make the Hoosier soccer team one of the best in the nation.

The 1997 men's soccer team went though the season undefeated and untied (20–0–0), winning their sixth Big Ten championship. They advanced to their twenty-secondNCAA Tournament, defeating Butler in the first game by a score of 2 to 1 in the third overtime, following freshman Matt Funderberger's goal. They then defeated Bowling Green 4 to 0, and South Florida 6 to 0. In the Final Four for the eleventh time, IU was defeated in the semi-final game by UCLA (the eventual champion) in the third (sudden-death) overtime, by a score of 1 to 0.

Women's Track and Cross Country

Roseann Barnhill, a freshman walk-on at IU in the fall of 1980, set two track records during her career, qualified for the NCAA cross country championship meet, and served as captain of the cross country team her junior and senior years. She graduated from IU in 1984, then earned an MS in exercise physiology in 1986. She worked as a graduate assistant at IU before serving as head coach at the University of Connecticut for three years. She became head coach at IU in 1989/90. Her cross country squads won the Big Ten in 1989 and 1990, and the women's track team won the Big Ten indoor title in 1991. Twenty-eight of her athletes have earned All-American honors.

IU women participated in track events as early as 1915. There was an extramural team in 1968 and 1969, sponsored by the Department of Physical Education for Women, but no financial assistance was available. The university began offering grants-in aid to women track and cross country athletes in 1978/79, when four women were given scholarships: Reba Jackson, Kelly Suellyn O'Toole, Denise Marie Sheire, and Karen Michelle Wechler. Forty-four coeds made up the teams. The following year, fifteen grants-in-aid were available.

Mark Witten was the first coach. Sam Bell served as coordinator during the first indoor and outdoor varsity seasons in both sports. Carol Stevenson coached both sports from the 1980/81 through the 1988/89 seasons; she was Coach of the Year in 1988. Roseann Barnhill Wilson, a 1984 IU graduate who lettered in both track and cross country, became the coach of the two squads in the fall of 1989. Bell continues to serve as coordinator.

The first Big Ten indoor track championship meet was held in Bloomington in 1982, and the first outdoor championships were held at the University of Illinois in Champaign. Wisconsin won the indoor meet, and Michigan State won the outdoor title. The Hoosiers have won the Big Ten indoor title two times, in 1988 and 1991, but have not captured an outdoor championship.

East Lansing, Michigan, was the site of the first Big Ten cross country meet, at which IU finished sixth in a field of ten. The Hoosiers won the Big Ten in 1989 and 1990 and were the runners-up in 1988. Colette Gourdeau was elected to the All-American cross country team in 1985. Kim Betz was the individual NCAA champion in 1987, followed by Michelle Dekkers in 1988. Dekkers also won the individual Big Ten title three years in a row: 1988, 1989, and 1990. Seven Hoosier coeds have earned Big Ten first team honors: Colette Gourdeau (1985–86), Kim Betz (1987), Toni Ann Angione (1988), Michelle Dekkers (1988–90), Mary Beth Driscoll (1989–90), Amy Legacki (1990), and Nicole Suever (1993). Coach Barnhill Wilson

Colette Gourdeau, shown here with coach **Carol Stevenson** at the end of a race, was considered IU's number one cross country runner in 1985, which was her first complete season; injuries had plagued her during her first two years. She was Indiana's first All–Big Ten and NCAA All-American cross country selectee in 1985. She also ran the mile and the 1,500 meter races, and was an NCAA 1,500 meter qualifier, but injuries kept her out of the competition. She was a Big Ten champion 3,000 meter runner in 1987 and 1988, and a 5,000 meter titlist in 1988.

was named the Big Ten Women's Indoor Track and Field and Cross Country Coach of the Year in 1991.

The Cream and Crimson female track and field stars have won sixty individual events and seven relays at the Big Ten meets. Among the outstanding athletes have been Mary C. "Tina" Parrott, IU's first female NCAA champion runner at 1,000 meters and an elite distance runner; Adrianne Diamond, an excellent performer in the 400 and 500 meter runs; dashers Reba Jackson and Heather Brown; long jumpers Regina Frye and DeDe Nathan; and javelin thrower and heptathlon competitor Carla Battaglia. Katrin Koch, a native of Germany, was a superb shot putter and discus thrower: she won the NCAA shot put title in 1992, won the Big Ten in both events in 1991 and 1992, and holds the conference record in those events; she was the 1992 recipient of the Big Ten Medal of Honor. Other stars in the distance runs have been cross country runners Kim Betz, Michelle Dekkers, Mary Beth Driscoll, Colette Gourdeau, and Amy Legacki.

In Big Ten competition, the IU women track and field team members have won forty-three individual championships and four relay races in the indoor meets since 1982, and thirty-four outdoor titles plus four relay victories.

Kim Betz became IU's first NCAA cross country champion when she ran the course in a record time of 16:11.0 in 1987. She was named to that year's All-American team and was awarded the Honda/Broderick Award as the nation's outstanding female collegiate athlete. Competing in the indoor track program, Betz placed second in both the mile and 3,000 meter runs. A leg injury prevented her from further competition.

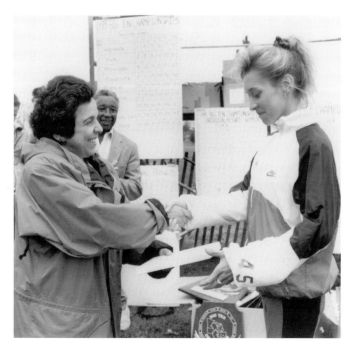

A native of South Africa, **Michelle Dekkers** moved to Texas with her family in 1985. She transferred to IU in 1988 from Northlake Junior College in Houston. Dekkers was one of Indiana's top distance runners, competing in cross country and track. During the 1988 season, she ran barefoot, winning her first Big Ten cross country title. She won the NCAA cross country crown that year, as Kim Betz had done the year before. In 1989, Dekkers won all but one of the seven cross country meets in which she participated; she finished third at the NCAA meet. She helped lead the IU women's cross country teams to Big Ten titles in 1989 and 1990, winning her third Big Ten crown in 1990.

A four-time All-American in track, Dekkers set the IU indoor 5,000 meter record in 1989. She finished third in the Big Ten indoor 5,000 meter run and second in the Big Ten outdoor 10,000 meter run. She is tied for second on IU's list in the mile run.

Dekkers is shown here at the 1989 Big Ten cross country championship meet in Madison, Wisconsin, receiving the championship plaque from Donna Shalala, then president of the University of Wisconsin, and now the secretary of Health and Human Services.

The Indiana University women's cross country team won its first Big Ten title on October 28, 1989, in Madison, Wisconsin. IU was led by Michelle Dekkers and Mary Beth Driscoll in the five kilometer course. Dekkers won in 16:19.1, followed by Driscoll in fourth, Kathy Gobbett in ninth, Amy Legacki in sixteenth, and Patricia Nelson in seventeenth. Debra Sauers and Melinda Maniatus also finished in the run. Dekkers won six meets during the year, with Driscoll finishing in the top five each time. The team was ninth in the NCAA meet, with Dekkers finishing third and Driscoll in eighteenth.

Kneeling, left to right: **Shannon Hoehn, Kristi Hill, Melinda Maniatus, Jenny Culberson, Kimberly Gerken, Kelly Woodman,** and **Jacquelyn Hoehn.** Standing: coach **Roseann Barnhill, Patricia Nelson, Michelle Dekkers, Esther Brooks, Mary Beth Driscoll, Kathy Gobbett, Amy Legacki, Deb Sauers, Kristen Ladkowski,** and coach **Sam Bell.**

Opposite: **Tina Parrott** was an outstanding sprinter in high school, but she switched to the longer distances at IU. As a sophomore, Parrott placed second in the 500 meter run at the Big Ten meet. She was the Big Ten indoor champion in the 600 yard run in 1984 and in the 800 meter run in 1985. She was the NCAA indoor 800 meter champion in 1985, finishing second in 1986. She won the Big Ten outdoor 800 and 1,500 meter runs in 1986, and was on the winning 4 x 400 meter relay team. As a senior, she competed in cross country. Parrott is shown here going into the bell lap of the 800 meter run at the 1986 Big Ten meet in Indianapolis. The other IU runner is **Kelly Greenlee.**

Adrianne Diamond is shown here receiving an award from Aline Robinson. Adrianne was a seven-time Big Ten 400 meter indoor and outdoor titlist in 1985, 1986, and 1987. In 1985 she won the Big Ten 400 and 500 meter runs and was part of the Big Ten champion 4 x 400 relay team. She was also a member of the NCAA champion 4 x 400 meter relay team.

DeDe Nathan, an All-Conference basketball and volley-ball player from South Side High School in Fort Wayne, Indiana, was named to the National High School All-American Track Team on three occasions. During her career at Indiana (1987–1990), she was a six-time All-American in track and an outstanding pentathlon performer. She won the Big Ten long jump title in 1988 and placed fourth at the NCAA meet. She won the 400 meter hurdle title in 1989 and 1990; in 1990 she also won the 55 meter hurdles, the pentathlon, and the long jump and was second in the heptathlon. Nathan won the heptathlon at the 1991 Pan American Games, and placed fourth in the heptathlon at the Olympic trials in 1992 and 1996.

Women's Soccer

Intramural and class soccer was played by IU coeds on the Dunn Meadow field prior to 1920. The popularity of the sport then waned on campus, and it was not until 1977 that a new women's soccer club was formed. By 1981, women's soccer was quickly becoming one of the fastest-growing college sports. That year 77 institutions of higher education had women's soccer teams; by 1996 there were 739 NCAA teams.

On June 10, 1992, the Indiana University Athletic Committee agreed to make women's soccer a varsity sport beginning in the 1993/94 season. Later that year, Joe Kelley, a former member of Coach Yeagley's squad, was made the team coach; he remains in that position today. Indiana's womens soccer athletes were first given grants-in-aid in 1993/94, when ten were awarded. The first intercollegiate women's soccer match featuring an IU team was played at the newly constructed Bill Armstrong Stadium on September 5, 1993, against the University of Cincinnati; IU won, 3 to 1. Big Ten competition started in 1994, and eight teams currently compete for honors in the sport: IU, Michigan, Michigan State, Minnesota, Northwestern, Ohio State, Penn State, and Wisconsin.

In the first four years of varsity play, the Hoosier women's soccer team under Coach Kelley compiled a record of 39–35–1 against all opponents, and 14–14–1 against Big Ten opponents. IU finished fourth in Big Ten play in 1995, losing in the semifinal match to Minnesota, the eventual Big Ten tourney winner, by a score of 3 to 2. The 1996 IU team had a season record of 11 and 11 going into the conference tournament. They came away with the Big Ten championship, holding their opponents scoreless in the three games. The Hoosier women advanced to the first round of the NCAA tournament that fall and were defeated in the first game by Notre Dame, which was ranked number one in the nation.

Midfielder Wendy Dillinger and goalkeeper Merit Elzey were named to the All–Big Ten team in 1994 and 1995, respectively. Other recent productive players have been Quincy Wolkowitz, Tracy Grose, Kris Fosdick, Amy Friederich, and Abby Ryan.

When women's club soccer returned to the campus in 1977 after an absence of many years, **Rita Stephens** was one of its outstanding players. She was the only member of the "no cut" club who could dribble with either foot.

Team Championships

BIG TEN CHAMPIONS

1914 Wrestling Team
1921 Wrestling Team
1921 Men's Tennis Team (C)
1924 Wrestling Team (C)
1925 Wrestling Team (C)
1925 Baseball Team
1926 Basketball Team (C)
1928 Basketball Team (C)
1928 Cross Country Team
1929 Cross Country Team
1930 Cross Country Team
1931 Wrestling Team
1931 Cross Country Team
1932 Wrestling Team
1932 Track Team (Indoor)
1932 Cross Country Team
1932 Baseball Team
1933 Wrestling Team
1934 Wrestling Team
1936 Wrestling Team
1936 Track Team (Outdoor)
1936 Basketball Team (C)
1938 Cross Country Team
1938 Basketball Team (C)
1939 Wrestling Team
1940 Cross Country Team
1940 Wrestling Team
1941 Basketball Team
1941 Track Team (Indoor and Outdoor)
1942 Cross Country Team
1943 Wrestling Team
1945 Football Team
1947 Cross Country Team (C)
1949 Baseball Team (C)

1950 Track Team (Outdoor)
1952 Tennis Team
1953 Tennis Team
1954 Basketball Team
1954 Tennis Team
1957 Basketball Team (C)
1957 Track Team (Indoor and Outdoor)
1958 Basketball Team
1961 Swimming Team
1962 Men's Golf Team
1962 Swimming Team
1963 Swimming Team
1964 Men's Tennis Team
1964 Swimming Team
1965 Swimming Team
1966 Swimming Team
1967 Football Team (C)
1967 Cross Country Team
1967 Swimming Team
1967 Basketball Team (C)
1968 Swimming Team
1969 Swimming Team
1968 Men's Golf Team
1970 Men's Golf Team
1970 Swimming Team
1970 Track Team (Outdoor)
1971 Track Team (Indoor)
1971 Swimming Team
1972 Cross Country Team
1972 Swimming Team
1973 Basketball Team
1973 Men's Golf Team
1973 Cross Country Team
1973 Swimming Team

NCAA CHAMPIONS

1932 Wrestling Team
1936 Cross Country Team
1938 Cross Country Team
1940 Basketball Team
1940 Cross Country Team
1942 Track Team
1942 Cross Country Team
1953 Basketball Team
1968 Swimming Team
1969 Swimming Team
1970 Swimming Team

1971 Swimming Team
1972 Swimming Team
1973 Swimming Team
1976 Basketball Team
1981 Basketball Team
1982 Soccer Team
1982 Women's Tennis Team
1983 Soccer Team
1987 Basketball Team
1988 Soccer Team

1973 Track Team (Indoor and Outdoor)
1974 Track Team (Indoor and Outdoor)
1974 Swimming Team
1974 Basketball Team
1974 Men's Golf Team
1975 Basketball Team
1975 Swimming Team
1975 Men's Golf Team
1975 Track Team
1976 Swimming Team
1977 Swimming Team
1978 Swimming Team
1979 Track Team (Indoor and Outdoor)
1979 Swimming Team
1980 Basketball Team
1980 Swimming Team
1980 Cross Country Team
1980 Track Team (Indoor)
1981 Basketball Team
1982 Women's Tennis Team
1983 Swimming Team
1983 Women's Softball Team
1983 Women's Tennis Team
1983 Track Team (Indoor)
1983 Basketball Team
1983 Women's Basketball Team (C)
1984 Women's Tennis Team
1984 Swimming Team
1984 Track Team (Indoor)
1985 Swimming Team
1985 Track Team (Indoor and Outdoor)
1985 Women's Tennis Team
1986 Women's Golf Team
1986 Women's Softball Team

1987 Basketball Team
1987 Women's Tennis Team
1987 Women's Golf Team
1988 Women's Track Team (Indoor)
1988 Women's Tennis Team
1989 Women's Cross Country Team
1989 Women's Tennis Team
1989 Basketball Team
1990 Women's Cross Country Team
1990 Women's Golf Team
1990 Women's Tennis Team
1990 Men's Track Team (Indoor and Outdoor)
1991 Basketball Team
1991 Men's Track Team (Indoor and Outdoor)
1991 Men's Soccer Team
1991 Women's Track Team
1991 Men's Golf Team
1991 Women's Tennis Team
1992 Women's Tennis Team
1992 Women's Golf Team
1992 Men's Soccer Team
1993 Men's Basketball Team
1993 Women's Tennis Team
1994 Women's Softball Team
1994 Men's Soccer Team
1994 Women's Tennis Team
1995 Women's Tennis Team
1995 Men's Soccer Team (C)
1995 Women's Golf Team
1996 Women's Golf Team
1996 Women's Soccer Team
1996 Men's Soccer Team
1997 Men's Soccer Team

A Chronology of Sports at IU

1867 Baseball club formed.

1883 IU plays its first intercollegiate athletic contest, losing the baseball game to Asbury College, 23 to 6.

1884 Campus moves to Dunn Meadow after fire on Seminary Campus.

1886 Football gridiron built at Seminary Campus.

1887 IU loses its first intercollegiate football game, to Franklin College, 6 to 8.

1890 IU Tennis Association formed.

1892 First gymnasium constructed.

1894 Preston Eagleston becomes the first black member of an IU football team.

1896 New gymnasium constructed; later named Assembly Hall.

Big Seven or Western Conference formed.

1897 Women's basketball clubs begin exhibitions.

IU defeats Wabash College in its first track meet.

1898 Jordan Field first used for football, baseball, and track.

James Horne, IU football coach, is said to have invented the naked reverse.

1899 A 6-hole golf course is constructed between the Jordan River and 10th Street.

Dunn Meadow Golf Club formed.

IU joins the "Big Nine."

1900 Men's tennis team competes in the state meet at Irvington.

1901 IU loses its first intercollegiate basketball game, to Butler, 17 to 20.

Hare and Hound Club formed.

1903 Zora G. Clevenger is named IU's first All-American (football).

1904 George W. Thompson is the first black to compete as a member of the IU track team.

Leroy Samse and Tad Shideler each win silver medals at the Olympic Games (IU's first Olympic medals).

1905 Women's intramural tennis begins.

1906 Leroy Samse sets new world record in the pole vault.

New tennis courts open east of Mitchell Hall.

The precursor of the NCAA is formed.

1910 IU's football team does not allow the goal line to be crossed all season.

First planned Homecoming game, vs. Illinois.

1911 First letter in wrestling awarded.

Booster Club organizes the first state high school boys' basketball championship.

1912 Ohio State joins the "Big Ten."

Sigma Delta Psi athletic honorary society formed.

1913 "I" Men's organization formed.

Women's Athletic Association formed on campus.

1914 IU wins its first Big Ten title (wrestling).

IU gymnasts (four men) enter Big Ten meet in Chicago.

Women's swimming made part of the Women's Athletic Association program.

1915 Matthew Winters is first winner of Big Ten Medal of Honor.

Gimbel Award is initiated.

IU ties Iowa for Big Ten wrestling title.

1916 Ground is broken for new gym on 7th Street.

1917 Swimming events are held in Student Building or Assembly Hall.

Athletic Conference of American College Women started.

Women's soccer club formed.

First basketball game in new gymnasium (Jan. 19).

1919 Mary Deputy is first Maxwell Award winner.

Sigma Rho Tau honorary swimming fraternity founded.

1920 Men swimmers participate in first intercollegiate meet.

1921 IU co–Big Ten tennis champs with Chicago.

Tennis player Fred Bastion wins Big Ten singles title.

IU wins its third Big Ten wrestling title.

Everett S. Dean is IU's first All-American in basketball.

1923 Zora G. Clevenger becomes athletic director.

Swimmers and divers participate in IU's first Big Ten meet.

Ground is broken for new stadium on 10th Street.

1924 Wrestlers win their fourth Big Ten title.

Varsity golf team formed.

1925 Everett S. Dean becomes head coach in baseball and basketball.

Billy Hayes becomes head coach in track and cross country.

10th Street Memorial Stadium is dedicated (Nov. 21).

First Old Oaken Bucket game.

Wrestlers win their fifth Big Ten crown.

1926	Baseball team wins its first Big Ten championship.
	Basketball team is co-champion of the Big Ten with Iowa, Michigan, and Purdue
	Harlan "Pat" Page becomes head football coach.
1927	Billy Thom becomes head wrestling coach.
1928	Basketball team shares its second Big Ten crown with Purdue.
	Cross country team wins its first Big Ten title.
	New Fieldhouse is dedicated (Dec. 12).
1929	Men win their second Big Ten cross country meet.
	Golfers win state intercollegiate meet.
	Balfour Award is initiated.
1930	Men win their third Big Ten cross country meet.
1931	Wrestlers win their sixth Big Ten crown.
	IU wins its fourth Big Ten cross country meet.
	Billy Hayes takes over as head football coach.
1932	Robert Royer becomes head swimming coach.
	IU wins NCAA wrestling title.
	Wrestlers win their seventh Big Ten title.
	Baseball team wins its second Big Ten title.
	Cross country team wins its fifth Big Ten title.
	Track team wins its first indoor Big Ten title.
1933	IU wins its eighth Big Ten wrestling crown.
	Track team wins its second Big Ten indoor meet.
	Golfers enter first full team in Big Ten meet.
1934	Wrestlers win their ninth Big Ten title.
	Bo McMillin becomes head football coach.
	Hugh E. Willis becomes golf coach.
1936	Cross country team sweeps National AAU meet.
	Wrestlers win their tenth Big Ten crown.
	IU wins its first Big Ten outdoor title.
	Women swimmers participate in meets in Indiana and Detroit.
	Men win their third Big Ten basketball championship (shared with Purdue).
1938	IU wins its first NCAA cross country championship.
	Men win their sixth Big Ten cross country meet.
	IU shares Big Ten baseball title with Iowa.
	Branch McCracken succeeds Everett S. Dean as head basketball coach.
	Paul "Pooch" Harrell succeeds Dean as baseball coach.
1939	Wrestlers win their eleventh Big Ten title.
1940	IU wins its first NCAA basketball championship.
	Cross country team wins its second NCAA.
	IU wins its seventh cross country championship.
	Wrestlers win their twelfth Big Ten title.
1941	IU wins its third Big Ten basketball title.
	Track team wins its third indoor and second outdoor Big Ten titles.
1942	IU is the NCAA track champion.
	IU wins its third NCAA cross country championship.
	Cross country team wins its eighth Big Ten title.
	Men's gymnastics team returns to Big Ten competition.
1943	Wrestlers win their thirteenth Big Ten title.
1945	IU wins its first Big Ten football championship.
	Gordon Fisher becomes track and cross country coach.
1946	IU shares its ninth Big Ten cross country title with Wisconsin.
	Charlie McDaniel succeeds Billy Thom as wrestling coach.
1948	Clyde Smith becomes head football coach after

	McMillin retires.
1949	IU shares the Big Ten baseball crown with Iowa and Michigan.
	Dale Lewis is named tennis coach for the men.
	Ernie Andres becomes baseball coach.
1950	Track team wins its third outdoor Big Ten crown.
1951	Baseball diamond is built near Fee Lane and East 13th Street; named Sembower Field in 1960.
1952	Men's tennis team wins its second Big Ten title.
	Bernie Crimmins succeeds Smith as football coach.
1953	Basketball team wins its second NCAA championship.
	IU wins its fourth Big Ten basketball title.
	Tennis team wins its third Big Ten crown.
1954	Basketball team wins its fifth Big Ten basketball title.
	Tennis team wins its fourth Big Ten title.
1955	Men's soccer club is started.
1956	Dick Albershardt wins NCAA trampoline title.
1957	IU shares Big Ten basketball title (its sixth) with Michigan State.
	Track team wins its fourth indoor and fourth outdoor Big Ten crowns.
	New IU golf course opens.
1958	James "Doc" Counsilman succeeds Robert Royer as swimming coach.
	Robert Fitch becomes head golf coach.
	Bill Landin becomes tennis coach.
	Phil Dickens becomes football coach.
	Basketball team wins its seventh Big Ten title.
	Construction begins on new football stadium at Dunn and 17th Streets.
1959	Last football game is played at 10th Street Memorial Stadium (Nov. 7); Purdue wins, 10 to 8.
	Hobie Billingsley becomes IU's first diving coach.
1960	New football stadium is dedicated (Oct. 22).
	New Fieldhouse at Fee Lane and 17th Street is dedicated (Dec. 3).
1961	School of HPER building is constructed.
	Men win their first Big Ten swimming crown—the first of 20 straight.
1962	Men win their first Big Ten golf meet.
	Swimmers win their second Big Ten title.
	Billy Hayes track is dedicated (Jan. 11).
	Pool in HPER is named in honor of Robert Royer (Mar. 3).
	James Lavery succeeds Gordon Fisher as track and cross country coach.
	Kay Burrus is named coach of women's field hockey team; first varsity team is formed.
	Women's basketball goes extramural.
1963	Swimmers win their third Big Ten crown.
	Clevenger Service Award is initiated.
	Jerry Yeagley joins faculty and becomes coach of soccer club.
1964	Men win their fifth Big Ten tennis title.
	Swimmers win their fourth Big Ten championship.
1965	Lou Watson succeeds McCracken as head basketball coach.
	John Pont becomes head football coach.
	Swimmers win their fifth Big Ten title.
1966	Swimmers win their sixth Big Ten title.
	Women's volleyball starts.

1967   IU shares Big Ten football championship with Minnesota and plays in the Rose Bowl: USC 13, IU 3.
Men win their tenth Big Ten cross country meet.
Men swimmers win their seventh Big Ten title.
Basketball team shares Big Ten title (its eighth) with Michigan State.
Women participate in first intercollegiate tennis match.
Women's golf team starts.
Women's gymnastics team starts.

1968   Men swimmers win their first of six straight NCAA titles.
Men swimmers win their eighth Big Ten title.
Men golfers win their second Big Ten meet.
Women's varsity golf begins.
Women's varsity softball starts.
Women's swimming and diving becomes a varsity sport.

1969   Swimmers win their second NCAA and their ninth Big Ten championship.
Sam Bell becomes head coach of track and cross country.
Hobie Billingsley becomes coach for women's diving team.

1970   IU swimmers win their third NCAA title and their tenth Big Ten title.
Golfers win their third Big Ten title.
Trackmen win their fifth outdoor Big Ten title.
Last basketball game is played in 17th Street Fieldhouse.

1971   IU wins its sixth outdoor Big Ten track title.
Swimmers win their fourth NCAA title and their eleventh Big Ten crown.
Women swimmers win unofficial Big Ten title.
Bob Knight is named basketball coach to succeed Watson.
First basketball game is played in the New Assembly Hall (Dec. 3).
Basketball court is named McCracken Court (Dec. 18).
Bea Gorton is named women's basketball coach.

1972   Men win their tenth Big Ten cross country title.
Men swimmers win their fifth NCAA title and their twelfth Big Ten title.
Women swimmers win their second unofficial Big Ten crown.
Scott Greer becomes men's tennis coach.
Doug Blubaugh succeeds McDaniel as wrestling coach.
Congress amends the Higher Education Act of 1965; its Title IX revolutionizes women's intercollegiate athletics.

1973   Leanne Grotke is named first women's athletic director.
Jerry Yeagley becomes varsity soccer coach as the team becomes a varsity sport.
Bob Lawrence assumes baseball coaching duties.
Lee Corso replaces Pont as football coach.
Men win their eleventh Big Ten cross country title.
Men golfers win their fourth Big Ten crown.
Basketball team wins its ninth Big Ten title.
Men win their sixth straight NCAA swim crown and their thirteenth straight Big Ten title.
Track team wins both Big Ten indoor and outdoor meets.

1974   IU wins both indoor and outdoor track titles.
Swimmers finish 2nd in NCAA, but win their fourteenth straight Big Ten title.
Men's basketball team wins first and only CCA title.

Men win their tenth Big Ten basketball title.
Golfers win their fifth Big Ten meet.

1975   IU wins its eleventh Big Ten basketball title.
Swimmers finish 2nd in the NCAA, but win their fifteenth Big Ten title.
Men golfers win their sixth Big Ten title.
Track team wins its seventh Big Ten crown.
Ann Lawver is named volleyball coach.
Louetta Bloecher is named women's softball coach.
Don Glass is named women's swim coach.
Dean Summers becomes women's tennis coach.

1976   IU basketball team wins its third NCAA championship and its twelfth Big Ten championship.
Men swimmers win their sixteenth Big Ten title.
Ann Lawver is named women's softball coach.
Joy Malchodi is named women's basketball coach.

1977   IU swimmers win their seventeenth straight Big Ten title.
Lin Loring becomes women's tennis coach.
Pat Fabozzi is named field hockey coach.

1978   Swimmers win their eighteenth straight Big Ten title.
Women's varsity track team starts.
Pete Murao wins NCAA floor exercise championship.
Mark Witten is named women's track and cross country coach.

1979   IU wins Big Ten indoor and outdoor track titles.
Swimmers win their nineteenth Big Ten title.
Men's basketball team wins the NIT.
Ann Lawver is named interim women's athletic director.
Gayle Blevins is named softball coach.
Women's varsity cross country begins.
Pat Barry becomes women's swim coach.

1980   Men win their thirteenth Big Ten basketball title.
Swimmers win their twentieth Big Ten title.
Cross country team wins its thirteenth Big Ten meet.
Men win their tenth indoor track title.
Isabella Hutchison becomes women's athletic director.
Women swimmers win their third unofficial Big Ten title.
Carol Stevenson is named women's track and cross country coach.

1981   Soccer stadium is built next to Billy Hayes Track.
Big Ten begins conference competition in women's sports.
Men's basketball team wins its fourth NCAA title and its fourteenth Big Ten title.
Sam Carmichael becomes coach of the women's golf team.
Maryalyce Jeremiah becomes women's basketball coach.
Monon Spike rivalry with Purdue in volleyball starts.
Steve Greco becomes men's tennis coach.

1982   Men's soccer team wins its first NCAA championship.
Women's tennis team wins its first NCAA and first Big Ten titles.
First Big Ten women's track and cross country meets are held.
Women's field hockey is discontinued as a varsity sport.
Men's gymnastics is discontinued as a varsity sport.
Bob Bruce becomes women's swim coach.

1983   Men's soccer team wins its second NCAA title.
Men swimmers win their twenty-first Big Ten title.

Women's softball team wins Big Ten championship.

Women win their second Big Ten tennis title.

Men win their tenth Big Ten indoor track meet.

Men win their fifteenth Big Ten basketball championship.

Women share the Big Ten basketball title with Ohio State.

Soccer stadium is named Bill Armstrong Stadium.

Doug West is named women's volleyball coach.

Sam Wyche takes over as football coach.

1984 Women win their third Big Ten tennis title.

Women's gymnastics is discontinued as a varsity sport.

Men swimmers win their twenty-second Big Ten title.

Men win their eleventh indoor Big Ten track title.

Bob Morgan becomes baseball coach.

Bill Mallory succeeds Wyche as football coach.

1985 Men win their twelfth indoor and tenth outdoor Big Ten track titles.

Men swimmers win their twenty-third Big Ten title.

Women win their fourth Big Ten tennis title.

Jorja Hoehn becomes women's basketball coach.

Jim Humphrey takes over as wrestling coach.

1986 Women win their first Big Ten golf title.

Women win their second Big Ten softball championship.

Ken Hydinger becomes men's tennis coach.

Chet Jastremski is named women's swim coach.

1987 Men win IU's fifth NCAA and sixteenth Big Ten championships in basketball.

Women win their fourth Big Ten tennis title.

Women win their second Big Ten golf title.

Diane Stephenson is named women's softball coach.

Tom Shoji is named women's volleyball coach.

1988 Men's soccer team wins its third NCAA championship.

Women win their first Big Ten indoor track title.

Women win their fifth Big Ten tennis title.

Jim Izard is named women's basketball coach.

1989 Women win their first Big Ten cross country title.

Women win their sixth Big Ten tennis title.

Men win their seventeenth Big Ten basketball title.

I Women's Association formed, with 190 charter members.

Bill Fitch retires; Sam Carmichael is named men's golf coach.

Jeff Huber succeeds Hobie Billingsley as men's and women's diving coach.

Sam Bell assumes women's track and cross country coaching duties.

Roseann Barnhill leads women's cross country team.

Joe McFarland becomes wresting coach.

1990 Women win their second Big Ten cross country meet.

Women win their third Big Ten golf title.

Women win their seventh Big Ten tennis title.

Men win their thirteenth indoor and their eleventh outdoor Big Ten track title.

James "Doc" Counsilman retires as swimming coach.

1991 Men win their eighteenth Big Ten basketball title.

Men win their fourteenth indoor and their twelfth outdoor Big Ten track titles.

Soccer is added to Big Ten competition.

IU wins the first Big Ten soccer title.

Women win their second Big Ten track title.

Men win their seventh Big Ten golf title.

Women win their eighth Big Ten tennis title.

Kris Kirchner succeeds Counsilman as swim coach.

Jill Sterkel is named women's swim coach.

1992 Women win their ninth Big Ten tennis title.

Women win their fourth Big Ten golf title.

Women's soccer becomes a varsity sport.

Men win their second Big Ten soccer title.

Nancy Nitardy is named women's swim coach.

Duane Goldman is named wrestling coach.

1993 Men win their nineteenth Big Ten basketball title.

Women win their tenth Big Ten tennis title.

Joe Kelley is named women's soccer coach.

Katie Weismiller is named women's volleyball coach.

1994 Women win their third Big Ten softball title.

Women win their eleventh Big Ten tennis title.

Men win their third Big Ten soccer title.

1995 Women win their twelfth Big Ten tennis title.

Men's soccer team shares Big Ten soccer title with Wisconsin.

Women win their fifth Big Ten golf title.

Counsilman Aquatic Center and Billingsley Diving Center are opened in the Student Recreational Sports Center.

Mary Ann Rohleder succeeds Isabella Hutchison as women's athletic director.

1996 Women win their sixth Big Ten golf title.

Men's basketball team wins the pre-season NIT.

Mellencamp Pavilion is dedicated.

Roseann Barnhill-Wilson becomes women's track coach.

Women win Big Ten soccer tourney.

Men win their fifth Big Ten soccer tourney.

17th Street Fieldhouse is renovated, is named Harry Gladstein Fieldhouse.

1997 Robert S. Haugh Track and Field Complex is dedicated.

Men's and women's NCAA track and field championships are held at the new complex.

Cam Cameron replaces Bill Mallory as football coach.

Women athletes who played on IU teams from 1960 to 1977 are retroactively awarded "I" letters (June 14).

Men's soccer team wins its sixth Big Ten championship.

Name Index

Abernethy, Tom, 85, color insert
Abram, Karna, 126, 130
Ackerman, Bob, 119
Adams, Don, 125
Aguilar, Vilma, 156
Ahamed, Zahra, 149
Albershardt (Albers), Dick, 98, 100
Albohm, Marg, xix
Alcini, Amy, 150
Aldridge, D. E., 96
Alford, Steve, xix, 92, 93, color insert
Allen, Wendy, 149
Amberg, Sue, 147
Anderson, Don, 49
Anderson, Eric, color insert
Anderson, Jim, 49
Andres, Ernie, 8, 10, 68, 73
Angione, Toni Ann, 167
Applegate, Earl, 52
Archer, Chris, 133
Armbrustmacher, Liz, 138, 140
Armendarez, Monica, 154, color insert
Armstrong, Paul, 69
Artz, Kelly, 156
Atkinson, David, 45
Atwater, M. D., 2

Bailey, Damon, color insert
Bain, Carol, 148
Balfour, Lloyd G., xvi, xvii, xviii
Bankston, Jeff, 113
Barnes, Ken, 49
Barnes, Quacy, 126, color insert
Barnhill-Wilson, Roseann, 167, 170, color insert
Barrett, Eric, 59, color insert
Barry, Pat, 156
Barton, William, 110
Bastion, Fred, 57, 58
Bateman, Bryan, 113
Bates, R. C., 122
Battaglia, Carla, 169
Bayles, Dave, 113
Beaver, Richard, 110
Beckner, Art, 66
Beeler, Dale, 98
Beggs, Jill, 138
Behringer, Herb, 165
Bell, Greg, 44, 45, 50
Bell, Sam, 44, 167, 170, color insert
Bellamy, Walt, 67, 68, 81

Belshaw, Ed, 96
Belshaw, George, 96
Benbrook, Al, xiv
Bender, Bob, 85
Bennett, Charles E., xvii, 7, 18, 19
Benson, Kent, 85, 86, 88
Bernauer, Ed, 49
Berndt, Cotton, 14, 15, 17
Berryhill, Coach, 2
Betancourt, Armando, 161
Betner, Donna, 142
Betz, Kim, 167, 169
Biddinger, Gary, 119
Billingsley, Hobie, 106, 109, 110, 113, 156
Binkley, James, 59
Bittermuer, C., 148
Blab, Uwe, color insert
Blevins, Gayle, 153, 154
Bloecher, Louetta, xix, 137, 152, 154
Blubaugh, Doug, 94
Bodenhafer, Walter B., 94
Bodger, Emily, color insert
Boehm, Jack, 110
Bollinger, Rob, 109
Bolyard, Tom, 68
Boncet, Dave, 163
Borowski, Steve, 113
Bostic, Rachelle, 126, 128, 129
Bouchie, Steve, 89, 91
Boyd, Alonzo, 122, 124
Boyer, Ron, 120
Bradley, Steve, color insert
Brahm, Terry, 45
Brandt, Kellie, color insert
Braughler, Matt, 8
Brawner, Melissa, color insert
Breen, George, 107
Brocksmith, Henry, 43, 54, 55
Brooks, Esther, 170
Brown, Christy, 154
Brown, Eddie, 49
Brown, Heather, 169
Brown, Howard, 23, 26, 29
Brown, Jim, 98
Brown, Tony, 89
Bruce, Bob, 156
Bruening, Hilary, color insert
Brunoehler, Dick, 105
Bryan, Charlotte Lowe, 1
Bryan, William L., 1, 3, 20, 66

Bryant, Shirley, 126, color insert
Buckner, Quinn, 85, 87, color insert
Bumgarner, Cindy, 126, 130
Burke, Beth, 156
Burks, Steve, 159, 166
Burnett, Bob, 46
Burrell, Bill, 113
Burrus, Kay, xix, 133, 134
Burton, Roger, 122
Buse, Mark, 45, color insert
Bush, H. T., 96
Bush, Leslie, 113, 156, 157
Bustard, Cynthia, 133
Butcher, Jade, 23, 33, 35
Butler, Evelyn, 133
Buzminski, Angela, 146
Byers, Herman, 66
Byers, Phil, 66, 73
Bynum, Kelly, 128

Calloway, Rick, 92, color insert
Cameron, Cam, 23
Camp, Walter, xiii
Campbell, Jannette, color insert
Campbell, Milt, 44, 45, 50
Cannady, John, 23, 27
Capron, John C., xii
Carlton, Nick, 113
Carmichael, Sam, 142, 143, 144, 146, color insert
Carney, Erin, color insert
Cartwell, Jennifer, color insert
Cass, William, 110
Cave, George, 105
Cellini, O. G., 96
Cerroni, Tony, color insert
Chambers, Goethe, 73
Chandler, Roger, 96, color insert
Chapman, Tracy, 142, 143
Cheaney, Calbert, color insert
Cheney, Jim, 121
Chesstal, Barb, 135
Childs, Clarence, 17, 43, 45
Chirichetti, Lisa, 143
Christopherson, Jane, 127
Chubb, Nancy, 133, 135
Ciolli, Frank, 27
Cisco, Steve, 121
Cleaver, G. C., 18
Clements, Cindy, 133
Clevenger, Zora, xvi, 14, 16, 20, 21, 22

Cecil K. Byrd (1913–1997), an Indiana University librarian, teacher, and university president, had a long and distinguished record of service to the university. He edited *Frank M. Hohenberger's Indiana Photographs* and co-authored (with Dorothy C. Collins) *Indiana University: A Pictorial History,* both published by Indiana University Press.

Ward W. Moore is a native of Cowden, Illinois, and earned three degrees at the University of Illinois in Urbana. He is a Professor Emeritus of Physiology and Biophysics and, at the time of his retirement, was an Associate Dean of the Indiana University School of Medicine and Director of its Medical Sciences Program.